Praise for *Ravenous*

*"Food as protection, comfort, pleasure, and love,
a defense against deprivation, a buffer against pain
—so many of us will recognize our insatiable hungers
in Dayna Macy's quest to understand her own. But the
real appeal of **Ravenous** is Macy's voice: her candor
and humility; her curious mind and storyteller's clarity;
and the open, generous heart she brings to her tale of
learning to find peace with her appetite and her body."*

— **Kate Moses**, author of *Cakewalk*

*"**Ravenous** is among the most engaging, fun, and insightful
books about appetite you'll ever read. A wonderful mélange
of memoir (what a family!), recipes (you can taste them),
the exploration of food production (slow, local, artisanal,
organic) topped off by uncommonly delicious writing."*

— **Sue Halpern**, author of *Can't Remember What I Forgot*

*"This rich, compelling book follows a woman's
search for balance, and ultimately, freedom, in her
relationship to food. Macy's writing is strong and
beautiful, every page filled with risk and integrity.
I truly loved **Ravenous**. It's a real accomplishment."*

— **Kim Chernin**, author of *In My Mother's House*

*"**Ravenous** is the journey of a courageous, smart,
beautiful woman who learned that there is no final
answer—but that the inquiry itself, the work of being and
growing and accepting, is the salve that heals the heart.
Macy's writing is the perfect blend of humor, irony, and
wit. Her warmth and earnestness is so lovable that I found
myself rooting for her all along. I couldn't put it down!"*

— **Stephanie Snyder**, yoga instructor and
creator of *Yoga for Strength and Toning*

Ravenous

Ravenous

A Food Lover's Journey
from Obsession to Freedom

Dayna Macy

HAY HOUSE, INC.

Carlsbad, California • New York City
London • Sydney • Johannesburg
Vancouver • Hong Kong • New Delhi

Published and distributed in the United States by: Hay House, Inc.:
www.hayhouse.com • *Published and distributed in Australia by:*
Hay House Australia Pty. Ltd.: www.hayhouse.com.au • *Published
and distributed in the United Kingdom by:* Hay House UK, Ltd.: www
.hayhouse.co.uk • *Published and distributed in the Republic of South
Africa by:* Hay House SA (Pty), Ltd.: www.hayhouse.co.za • *Distributed
in Canada by:* Raincoast: www.raincoast.com • *Published in India by:*
Hay House Publishers India: www.hayhouse.co.in

Design: Tricia Breidenthal

"The Breeze at Dawn" (p. 156), "The Seed Market" (p. 163), and "A
Great Wagon" (p. 167) from *The Essential Rumi,* by Jalal al-Din Rumi,
translated by Coleman Barks (HarperOne, 1997). © Coleman Barks.
Used by permission of the translator.

The author of this book does not dispense medical advice or
prescribe the use of any technique as a form of treatment for physical,
emotional, or medical problems without the advice of a physician,
either directly or indirectly. The intent of the author is only to offer
information of a general nature to help you in your quest for emotional
and spiritual well-being. In the event you use any of the information
in this book for yourself, which is your constitutional right, the author
and the publisher assume no responsibility for your actions.

Some names have been changed to protect privacy.

Library of Congress Cataloging-in-Publication Data

Macy, Dayna.
  Ravenous : a food lover's journey from obsession to freedom / Dayna
Macy.
     p. cm.
  ISBN 978-1-4019-2691-5 (hardcover : alk. paper) 1. Macy,
Dayna--Psychology. 2. Overweight persons--United States--Biography.
3.
Reducing diets. 4. Natural foods. 5. Compulsive eating. 6. Food
habits--Psychological aspects. 7. Weight loss. I. Title.
  RC628.M335A3 2011
  616.85'26--dc22
  [B]
                                         2010029887

Hardcover ISBN: 978-1-4019-2691-5
Digital ISBN: 978-1-4019-3085-1

14   13   12   11   4   3   2   1
1st edition, February 2011

Printed in the United States of America

For my mother, Estelle Bogoff Macy
In memory of my father, Gilbert Macy

*"And all that huge
change came about
as I had the marzipan
in my mouth,
before I'd even swallowed it.
A taste—a memory—a landslide . . ."*

— PHILIP PULLMAN, *THE AMBER SPYGLASS*

Contents

Introduction

I'm in a gourmet food store near my Berkeley, California, home. White serving dishes, filled with a dozen kinds of olives, gleam behind the counter. The variety is dazzling—bright green Cerignolas, pinkish-brown Hondroelias, and almost-black dry-cured Moroccans.

The olives are for a dinner party I'm giving later in the week. I choose several varieties, scooping them into a container. When it's filled to the brim, I pay and leave.

I love olives. But I tell myself not to eat any: They're for the party. Also, they are little caloric bundles. And at 48, 5'6", and a size 18, I shouldn't binge.

I get in the car to drive home. I try to ignore the container on the seat next to me. But I can't resist. I taste a Cerignola first—it's large and piquant. I eat a Hondroelia next—meaty and satisfying. And the Moroccan? The salt bomb of my dreams. I eat a couple, then a few more, and then a few more.

By the time I get home, the olives are gone.

• • •

For as long as I can remember, I've turned to food for comfort.

I am ten. My parents have had another fight. My father packs his bag and says he's leaving.

"Where?" I ask, crying.

"Anywhere but here," he replies.

He grabs his suitcase and walks toward the door. Terror overrides my pride, and I grab onto his pants leg and scream, "Don't go! Don't leave us!"

He continues walking, dragging me with him, the burnt-orange shag carpet chafing my arms. He gives his leg a final shake. I lose my grip, and he walks out the door.

I lie on the floor for a few moments. Then I pick myself up and make my way to the kitchen. I open a can of black olives and put one on each finger of my left hand. One by one I eat them off each fingertip. When all five are gone, I pop another five onto my fingers and repeat the process until I've eaten them all.

But I'm not done. Next I heat up a package of 15 frozen assorted mini-pizzas in the oven. I eat the plain cheese, my least favorite, first; then the sausage; then the pepperoni. I'm stuffed, and I finally feel safe.

• • •

It's five years later, and I'm 15, babysitting for the nice family around the corner from my house. The kids are sleeping, and I start trolling around their refrigerator for something to eat. Then I spot it, the Holy Grail: a package of ham, which, because it's pork, I'm not allowed to eat at home.

I take out a slice of white bread, slather it with mustard, and throw on two pieces of ham. I gobble it quickly, as if expecting to be caught at any moment. When I'm done, I clean up, go back into the living room, and try to read a magazine. Two minutes later, I again hear the siren call. I go back to the kitchen and eat another sandwich.

Hoping they don't discover my crime for at least a few days, I finish the last of my neighbors' ham.

• • •

From 18 to 26, my weight stays a stable size 10. Through college, where I fall in love with a long-haired boy and during which time my brother has a mental breakdown and my father has a heart transplant; through graduate school, through a move to Switzerland for a romance, through my father's death at age 56, and through several years of living in New York before moving to California. Still not the size 4 of my skinny, flat-chested sister, but good enough.

• • •

I'm 28 and eating lunch at the iconic Chez Panisse restaurant, in Berkeley. I moved from New York to California earlier that year, ostensibly for a guy but really for the freedom that a new place promises. New York felt too choked with expectations of who I was supposed to be and who I was allowed to become. Many people come to New York to write. I left.

I order a dish of prosciutto-wrapped melon and sliced figs. It's served with a small mound of arugula topped with shaved Parmesan.

I have not yet heard the words *organic* or *sustainable agriculture*. I only know that this food, which dances in my mouth, tastes vibrant and alive; and I want to eat more of it in the future.

• • •

It's love. We lie in his bedroom in San Francisco and watch the fog hovering low, like a soft, downy blanket. I'm now 30. I know one day we'll marry. I can't quite accept that I am meant to be this happy; and though I don't understand it, I'm willing to take a leap of faith.

We celebrate our happiness with much food and drink. When we get married, I'm 33 and wear a size 12. If Scott notices, he doesn't say anything.

At our wedding reception in Napa, I eat the gorgeous roasted chicken and vegetables the restaurant has prepared. I wash it down with some great Cabernet—silk wedding dress be damned.

We cut our wedding cake; it's apricot eau-de-vie with butter-cream frosting. It's perfect. And though brides' appetites are often depicted as demure, I eat the entire slice.

• • •

While I work in book publishing by day, I begin writing essays for *Salon.com* and some magazines. In my spare time, I also take up yoga, which I find so difficult I hate it for the first six months of my practice. As my body begins to open, I get my first glimpse of its innate intelligence and begin to understand that it will tell me what it needs if I learn to listen.

From a co-worker, I hear about a Community Supported Agriculture project run by Full Belly Farm in Guinda, California. For ten bucks a week, I get a box of buoyant organic produce, usually picked the day before delivery.

I begin eating organic vegetables—kale, fennel, rutabaga, and more. Something in me gets happy when I eat this food.

I am 35 and wear a size 14.

• • •

It's the call I've been anticipating but also dreading, because I don't know what the news will be. "You're pregnant," the kind nurse says. "Twin boys, both healthy."

After I call Scott at work, I put on Dusty Springfield and start dancing around our living room.

I gain only 30 pounds during pregnancy—perhaps the result of being on bed rest for almost two months and delivering my sons at 32 weeks. When they are born, one weighs 5 pounds 3 ounces, the other 4 pounds 13 ounces.

"Linebackers," the neonatal nurse says.

"It's all that meat you ate," my doctor tells me.

After delivery, I'm 39 and wear a size 16.

• • •

I'm 41, and Matthew and Jack are almost two. I leave my job as head of publicity for *Salon.com* because I'm having a hard time juggling a heavy workload and raising small children.

I get a job running the communications department at *Yoga Journal* magazine and have the good fortune to be hired on the threshold of yoga's American renaissance.

While at one of the *Yoga Journal* conferences, I have the opportunity to practice with Patricia Walden, a master teacher. As she helps me move into a backbend, she asks, "Why are you in this body? What does your body have to teach you?" I wonder if she senses that this will become a defining question for me, one that I will wrestle with for much of the next decade.

I begin writing about food and spirituality for "Eating Wisely," the magazine's food column. I write on topics such as heirloom seeds, foraging, and Zen eating practices.

Over the next few years, I keep writing about eating wisely, but I can't help noticing the irony: while I am beginning to eat more wisely myself, I still eat too much and weigh too much.

• • •

I'm now 48. My husband, Scott, and I have been together for nearly 20 years. Our children are nine. I'm a size 18.

My relationship with food still doesn't work. Now I overeat daily, and overeating has become a habit.

In many ways, I have an addictive nature. In the past, I've dealt with my addictions by quitting them cold turkey: when I was 18, I put down my last cigarette. All or nothing always seems to have worked for me.

But I can't just give up food. And that makes things more complicated.

What should I eat? How should I eat it? How much should I eat? What does it mean to be nourished? How can I, a food lover, learn to eat in a balanced way?

I need to lose weight, and that usually means going on a diet. But I'm not going to do that. For starters, I've never wanted someone else telling me what to eat and when to eat it. But even more important, diets have always felt temporary to me. We talk about "going on" them, and that means we go off them, too. There's no middle ground. I want to find a balanced way of eating that I can live with for the rest of my life. If I can find that, my body will find the weight it wants to be. Balance, by its nature, cannot be all or nothing. Balance is not something you switch on or off. Balance is something you discover through experience—and continue to discover and hone as you move through life.

I'm not looking for a perfect body or a perfect way to eat. I am searching for a relationship with food that brings me greater health, peace of mind, and ease in my skin.

At midlife, I'm ravenous for something more than food. I'm hungry for freedom.

Part I
Seduction

I eat with gusto, damn, you bet.

— JONATHAN RICHMAN

Chapter 1

SAUSAGE

My father's haphazard "kosher" rules went something like this: Cheeseburgers? Yes. Shrimp? Okay, but only in Chinese restaurants. Pork? Forget about it. God would not only strike you dead for eating pig, he'd spit on you for good measure.

Naturally, then, I ate pork whenever possible—sometimes even with my mother.

Almost every Sunday while I was growing up, she'd take me to our local luncheonette, where we'd sit at the counter on brown Naugahyde-topped swivel stools. My mother ordered a buttered roll and coffee, and I got a ham sandwich on a kaiser roll with spicy mustard. I loved having not only my mother's full attention for an hour, but also her silent complicity in my crime.

This is what I'm remembering as I make my way to Berkeley's famed Café Rouge restaurant and meat market to make sausage with Scott Brennan, their charcutier.

Twenty pounds of Berkshire hog pork shoulder sit in a large metal vat, waiting to be ground into sausage. Brennan picks up a hunk, pointing out the glistening veins of well-marbled fat, which he says will make for an especially fine sausage.

Brennan pours several cups of sauvignon blanc over the meat, then adds a couple of tablespoons of chili flakes. He pulverizes a few heads of peeled garlic with a stone mortar and pestle and tosses them in. He retrieves a pan of toasted fennel seeds from the oven and starts to chop them with quick, efficient strokes.

He grabs some fresh herbs from the cooler, and before he rounds the corner, I already know he's got oregano—the herb's acrid, pungent scent precedes him. He flicks the oregano off the stem and begins to chop it together with some Italian parsley. He tosses the herbs into the meat vat along with a handful of coarse kosher salt.

"Why do you enjoy making sausage?" I ask as I watch him don latex gloves and begin mixing the meat, wine, and spices together.

He pauses and looks up. "It's so satisfying," he says. "It's such an old food." He dips his hands back into the meat. "What about you?"

I give him only half an answer. I tell him that I love this salty, fatty food. I tell him I want to learn how it's made so I can write more knowledgeably about a food I love.

I don't tell him about sneaking pork as a girl. Or that the spice-laden fat coating the roof of my mouth excites me. Or that I still think of sausage and its porcine cousins—ham and salami—as forbidden, which makes them all the more alluring.

Sausage is a food that seduces me. It's not the only one. There are a handful of foods that I long for—foods that, once I start eating them, I have a hard time stopping: Cheese. Olives. Chocolate. And sausage. They are my go-to foods, my fill-me-up-and-stuff-me foods. They all involve some combination of salt, fat, and sugar. They hold me captive.

If I'm ever going to regain my balance, I'm going to have to break the hold these foods have on me. I think I know how to do that: I will discover everything I can about them. I'll learn to make sausage. See how cheese is made and how the goats whose milk goes into the cheese are raised. Watch how chocolate confections are created. And see how olives, my favorite food in the world, are grown and then cured. Once I demystify the origins of these foods, perhaps I'll no longer be in their thrall.

• • •

It's a hot summer day in Montvale, New Jersey, circa 1970. I am ten years old, sitting on a curb outside Coiffures by Gigi, the salon where my mother is getting her blonde hair teased into a flip by Tom the hairdresser. The air is dense and muggy. Maple trees and weeping willows stand still in the stifling heat.

My ritual rarely varies. While my mother gets her hair done, I go to the nearby stationery store and buy a few Betty and Veronica comic books. Then I buy a five-pack of Slim Jims at the A&P supermarket. I sit on the curb outside the salon, open the red-and-yellow box, and take out the first stick. I open the comic book and begin to read, synchronizing bites with the words.

Bite. The outer skin pops as my teeth perforate the first layer. "Oh, Betty, you're not wearing *that?*" says the mean-spirited Veronica. Chew. A wad of grease explodes in my mouth. "Veronica, you are such a bitch!" says Betty. She actually doesn't say this, of course, but I wish she would. Veronica is a vain, petty tyrant; and I want Betty to knock her on her ass.

Bite. Greasy pulp again fills my mouth. "All the boys love me, Betty. Me!" screams Veronica. I swallow. I wish Betty would slug Veronica, but instead she just looks crestfallen. "Buck up, girl!" I want to yell. I can't bear to see her belittled by that shrew. I want her to learn to stand up for herself and to the bullies of the world. As I read on, I eat one Slim Jim after another, envisioning a different life for Betty.

As I do for me.

I know, even as I eat the entire box of Slim Jims, that this food is bad for me. But the combination of salt, fat, and sugar grabs me like metal to a magnet. As I chew the tough sticks, some of the anger, sadness, and bewilderment I feel about myself and my family abates.

I am lonely. I am convinced I was born into the wrong family. My father, when not being charming or sick, is a bully. He has, on various occasions, punished me by making me stand with my nose in the corner; washed my mouth out with Phisohex, an old-fashioned antibacterial soap; and hit me with a belt. I'm scared to be around him, which, it turns out, is a blessedly rare occurrence, since he travels six months a year on business. I don't know what he does, so I tell my friends he is an engineer. That sounds respectable, the kind of innocuous professional job that wouldn't invite any further questions.

"He made deals," my mother would later tell me, as if that explained everything. What kind? She didn't know. "How could you accept not knowing what your husband did for a living?" I recently asked her. "He had his life; I had mine," she said. I guessed later that his work had something to do with oil, since he traveled to Egypt, Saudi Arabia, and other countries where Jews had a hard time traveling. But to this day, I can't be sure.

He loves me. I often feel his warmth. But his love is dangerous and inconsistent.

My mother loves me, too, but I don't feel connected to her the way I want. As children often do, I want a mother who will mirror me. I want her to encourage my desire to write. I don't feel seen by her for who I am inside. Only from the vantage point of many decades do I now understand just how difficult her life with my father was and that it was her steely spine and commitment to her kids that kept our family intact.

My brother, whom I'll call David to protect his privacy, is three years older and has emotional problems. He's 6'5", withdrawn, and angry. I'm scared of him, and I know his problems are more profound than my family can or will admit.

My sister is sweet and does not rebel. She does not seem to live as messy a life as I do. She is six years older and inhabits what seems like a different universe. I feel afraid and anxious almost all the time. I don't know my place in the world and already know that my family cannot help me figure it out.

• • •

It's been decades since I've eaten Slim Jims; and now that I'm writing about them, I wonder how they'll taste and how I'll feel eating them again.

I go to my local 7-Eleven store and buy a five-pack from the counter. I glance around to see if anyone's watching. I quickly stuff the box into my purse. I feel like I'm buying porn.

I drive home and put the box on my desk. It sits there for days, until I finally decide it's time.

I unwrap the vacuum-packed foil seal. The vinegar smell hits me first. Then I take a bite. Salt, grease—a sensory bomb—just like I remember.

My nine-year-old son Jack walks into my office and sees the box. "Can I have one?" he asks.

I'm torn. If I eat Slim Jims, that's my choice. But give them to my son?

"Please?" he asks again.

I nod. For someone so young, he knows a lot about food. Since I never feed my kids food like this, part of me is curious to hear what he has to say.

I open one and hand it to him. He takes a bite. His eyes grow big.

"What do you think?" I ask.

He spews out a few words: "Oily. Greasy. Thick. Insanely salty. Chewy."

Then he adds: "It makes all the other food in my stomach seem boring, and it makes me want another one."

He's hit upon the magic formula for cheap, fast food. Grease, salt, and corn syrup, all thrown together to create a taste that makes you beg for more.

I want to see how it feels to eat them all, just like I used to. I eat a second, then a third, then a fourth.

Maybe it's a coincidence, but that night, I get sick. My body can't take it. I lie in bed, queasy, willing sleep to come.

• • •

Scott Brennan starts attaching parts to the meat grinder, a two-foot-long metal box that sits to the left of the butcher-block countertop where we've been working. He fishes them out of an ice bath, explaining that the parts need to be cold so that they will "retain chunks of fat." He attaches a 3/16-inch blade, which, he says, will keep the grind coarse, just big enough that the "connective tissue is ground down."

He attaches a makeshift guard to prevent the sausage from splattering on the wall. The workspace is pristine—the metal gleams, the yellow-and-green tile walls shine. He snaps on fresh latex gloves, grabs a hunk of the sausage mixture, and puts it into the metal tray on top of the grinder.

He turns the machine on, and after a few seconds, a combination of meat, fat, herbs, and spices starts to emerge from the blades. The smells of fennel and garlic predominate. The mixture starts to fill the metal tray that Brennan has placed at the base of the grinder. He kneads the sausage with his hands and shows me how nicely the fat smears.

After a few minutes, all 20 pounds of meat have been processed. Brennan then sets up the sausage press and inserts a stuffing tube on the bottom. He reaches below the counter into a small refrigerator and takes out a large vat marked "pig intestines." The intestines are wrapped around a plastic sheet with a top that opens up like a baggie to help load it onto the stuffing tube.

He takes out a sheet and fits it over the tube. He stuffs the sausage mixture into the large cylinder and starts pushing the meat down as he begins to turn the crank. The sausage makes its way into the casing.

He continues for a few minutes and there are now many feet of sausage, which he places in neat rows on a metal cooking sheet. They remind me of the ribbon candy of my youth, their curved corners making tight turns to form the next rows. Once the first layer is complete, he starts doubling them up.

The last of the 20 pounds of sausage makes its way out of the press. I watch Brennan grab a long-pronged fork and start poking occasional holes in the casings. "So the sausages don't explode when cooked," he says.

As he finishes up, I remember something I recently read: eating meats like sausage, which contain plenty of salt, fat, and sometimes sugar, contain drug-like compounds that have an opiate-like effect on the brain.

• • •

My father and I are home alone, which is rare. I'm 16. We sit at the table in our cheerful pink, yellow, and white kitchen, eating hot dogs and eggs. I always burn the hot dogs, on purpose. I love the taste of semicharred meat. My father suddenly drops his fork and clutches his chest. I know what's about to happen. He's having chest pains, and if his luck is bad, a heart attack.

He had his first heart attack while my mother was in the hospital giving birth to me. When I was growing up, his cardiologist made regular visits in the middle of the night. He'd take his stethoscope out of his black leather bag and listen to my father's chest, while the huge green metal oxygen tank that stood next to my father's bed pumped air into his nose.

As he clutches his chest I think, *I can't believe I'm the only one home.*

"Get the car," he croaks.

I have my driver's permit—but I've only taken a few laps around my old elementary-school parking lot and some sleepy side streets. I back our silver Grand Prix with its crimson crushed-velvet interior out of our garage and drive him to the hospital, speeding down the thruway at 70 miles an hour. Time seems to slow down. My only focus is the road ahead of me. We get there in 15 minutes.

I drive up to the emergency room and yell, "He's having chest pains!" The orderlies run out, strap him to a gurney, and take him inside. Turns out he was, in fact, having a heart attack. His third.

I somehow manage to drive home. My family is still not there. When I'm back in my kitchen, I start washing the dishes.

My father and I have such a complicated relationship. I both love and hate him. He can make me feel beautiful, special, and seen; or stupid, invisible, and dismissed. His moods change so quickly I feel the need to protect myself, insulate myself from him. Eating greasy, salty, fatty food literally pads me, thickens me from the inside out; and that extra padding helps me to feel safe. I suddenly begin to sob, the full impact of what's just happened starting to sink in. I grab one of the cold hot dogs abandoned a few hours earlier and begin to eat it. As I chew, I start to feel numb. I eat some more, until they are all gone.

• • •

It's time to twist the sausage. "Each link should be about a third of a pound," says Brennan. He picks up a seven-inch section of the long sausage tube and starts to twist it, flipping it forward in a little jump rope–like movement. He moves his hands down another seven inches and repeats the gesture, this time flipping the sausage backward, away from him. Forward, back, forward, back. Slowly, the sausage tube is transformed into remarkably uniform links.

As he continues this movement, I note that sausage making is physical—a lot of mixing, grinding, chopping, and stuffing. Brennan's job, however, is not limited to making sausage. He also answers phones and waits on customers while he makes his charcuterie. He is a gracious, compact perpetual-motion machine.

Finally, the sausages, all 50 of them, are twisted and then cut. He covers them with a sheet of butcher paper and slides the tray into the refrigerator below the workstation.

• • •

"You're aware, of course, that sausage is a phallic symbol?" a friend asks.

Yes, I am. In classic Freudian theory, it's common for a child to sexually desire the parent of the opposite sex. While it's true that my father was very handsome, with his silky, black, wavy hair and big, soft brown eyes, I didn't want to bed him—I wanted to deck him.

He lacked judgment and fairness in how he meted out punishment. He made me livid and then punished me if I expressed it. He gave me tender love with one hand and then withdrew it with the other. He traveled for six months a year and then waltzed back into our lives, resuming his despotic rule.

No, it's not sex I'm after, but justice. Just once when he was alive I wanted to hear him say he was wrong. That he was sorry. That he fucked up. But he never did.

• • •

Before I leave Café Rouge, I tell Brennan I want to buy some sausage for dinner.

In the meat case, trays of prime rib lie next to plates of rabbit pâté, duck-liver mousse, a round of mortadella, prosciutto, salamis, lard for cooking, and goat crépinettes. And sausage: boudin blanc, bratwurst, merguez, chorizo, and of course, the fennel sausage, which we've just made. I buy two of those.

When I get home, I pierce them, put them in a pan, and cook them up on the stove over a low heat, as Brennan suggested. My son Matthew doesn't eat sausage, nor does my husband, Scott, so as they eat their pizza and salad, I serve the sausages to Jack and myself, along with some raw sauerkraut, a slather of mustard, and a hunk of rye bread. It's a meal I could imagine my Polish and German Jewish great-grandparents eating— sans the pork, of course.

Jack and I cut into our sausage. "It's delicious," he says. He eats slowly, while I wolf mine down and it's gone. He puts his fork down and asks if he can clear his plate and leave the table.

"But you haven't finished," I tell him.

"I'm done," he tells me. He's no longer hungry. He's had enough.

Before he can take his plate off the table, I reach over and spear what's left on it.

Tuscan Kale with
White Beans and Sausage

Serves 4

8 ounces dried cannellini beans or 2 16-ounce cans
1 tablespoon good quality olive oil, plus extra for drizzling
2 well-spiced Italian sausages, diced (optional)
1 bunch of kale, stems and center veins removed,
    coarsely chopped (about 6 cups)
1 clove of garlic, minced (about 1 teaspoon)
½ teaspoon dried sage
½ cup chicken stock or vegetable stock
Salt and pepper to taste

If using dried beans, cover beans with cold water, bring
to a boil, turn off heat, and soak for an hour. Drain. Place
beans in pot with 8 cups salted water. Bring to a simmer
over high heat, reduce heat to medium-low, and simmer
1–1½ hours or until tender. Drain.

If using canned beans, simply drain and rinse.

Heat oil in large, heavy skillet over medium-high heat.
Add diced sausages and cook until lightly browned,
about 5 minutes. Remove from pan. Add kale and cook
3–4 minutes or until wilted but still crisp. Add sausage,
beans, garlic, sage, and stock and cook 3–4 minutes
more or until warmed through. Season to taste with salt
and pepper. Serve warm and drizzle with extra olive oil,
if desired. Makes about 5½ cups.

Chapter 2

CHEESE

I place a wedge of Cambozola, a triple-cream French blue cheese, on a plate. I cut some and spread it on a piece of fresh sweet baguette from Acme Bread Company, the Berkeley bakery that helped spark the artisan-bread movement. As I bite, my mouth sinks into the luscious, creamy texture of the cheese. I feel the crunch of the hot baguette as I taste the tang of the blue veins mingled with the sweet creaminess of the milk: perfection.

I wrap the cheese up and put it away, but instantly, it calls me back. I cut myself a little more, smear it on another bit of baguette, and repeat the experience. It is just as perfect. I do this again and again, until the wedge is gone.

I adore triple-cream cheeses like Cambozola and Brie. But once I start, I have a hard time stopping. My love for them is probably responsible for more than a few of my extra pounds. Which is why I'm now standing in the aging room of Redwood Hill Farm, a goat-cheese, kefir, and yogurt maker located in Sebastopol, about an hour north of San Francisco.

"Cheese making is an intimate conversation between the cheesemaker and the cheese," says Erika Scharfen, the head cheesemaker. I'm watching Erika and her assistant give a cider wash to the Gravenstein Gold, one of their seasonal raw-milk cheeses. The bright orange rinds cast an otherworldly glow, and the scents of goat milk and thyme fill the air. "The look of the milk tells me what its potential is and how I choose to work with it," she continues. "The end result is always a collaboration between me and the milk."

"Why did you become a cheesemaker?"

She pauses, then says, "Because of the smell. I remember when I was in college studying dairy production and processing, I visited several plants that were entirely mechanized and smelled like cold walk-in boxes. But then I visited Vella Cheese in Sonoma, and I liked the smells of the warm milk and of the wood in the aging rooms. I know most people don't have positive associations with the smell of mold, but to me it just smells right. It smells of nature, of things left undisturbed."

Erika tells me that cheese is made from just a few ingredients: milk; lactic-acid bacteria culture; rennet or another coagulant; salt; and in the case of surface-ripened cheeses (where the ripening process starts on the outside and progresses in), mold and yeast cultures. But it all begins with milk.

"I'm still in awe of the fact that in cheese making you start with essentially one ingredient—milk—and with not much else, create something so completely different," she says. "Liquid changes to solid, textures change as the solid curd ages, aromas and flavors change. All of the elements of a cheese are already in the milk. Time just moves these elements down a certain path."

• • •

I'm 11, and I want to write. I already have two important qualities a writer needs—a curious mind and a love of words. But I am still young enough to believe all artists are born, not made through hard work.

I want to write a book about a disaffected girl named Jill. She would run away from her suburban parents and live on the streets where, despite all odds, she would find a boyfriend who truly loved her. I take out a small stack of lined paper and write the title *Why Jill Why* and then stop. I'm nervous about writing, so I go into our kitchen to find something to soothe myself. I open the mustard-colored refrigerator. I ignore the Velveeta and Kraft singles, and then I see the foil-wrapped wedges of Laughing Cow cheese. I take the cheese back to my room; sit down on my thick, pink shag carpet; and pull the wedge's red tab down the center, splitting the foil apart. The cheese is soft and innocuous. I stick my finger in, dig some out, and lick it off.

I start writing the first line—I no longer remember what I wrote. Then immediately, I stop.

Who gave me permission to write? I think. *Who ever said I could?*

I stare at the mostly blank page; and after what seems like one very long moment, I make a decision that will limit my creative life for a long time to come: I put the paper back in the box and close the lid. Then I pick up the cheese, dig the rest of it out with my finger, and eat it.

It will be another 20 years before I figure out that eating can't replace creating. And that no one can give me permission to write except myself.

• • •

I leave Erika and make my way through the humming and whirring of the creamery floor. I walk past the cheese-making rooms with their enormous vats and draining tables, past the aging rooms full of yeasty smells, and up a flight of stairs to the office of Redwood Hill Farm's owner, Jennifer Bice.

Jennifer is a pioneer in the artisanal-cheese movement. She's been around goats her whole life, ever since her parents bought the land and moved her and her nine brothers and sisters from Los Angeles to Sebastopol in the late '60s. David Bice, one of Jennifer's brothers, who acts as our tour guide, tells us the farm started with just two goats. Today, the herd numbers around 350.

He leads me and two cheese buyers who are also on the tour into the center of the room, where I see a tasting table displaying many of the farm's award-winning cheeses. Jennifer invites us to dig in; and as we begin, she tells us that Redwood Hill is the first of five goat dairies in the United States that have qualified for the Certified Humane Raised and Handled label. This means, in part, that a third party has verified that the goats are raised with shelter, resting areas, and sufficient space to engage in natural behaviors, and that the goats' food contains no antibiotics or hormones.

The first cheeses we try are the fresh chèvres. They are fluffy, creamy, and a little dry. I especially like their softness and sourness.

We move on to the Crottin, a strong cheese with a wrinkly, slightly bitter rind. The Bucheret also has a bitter rind, but a thick, buttery inside. The interior of the cheese near the rind has turned a little gooey, which can happen as it ripens with age. I put some of the goo on a cracker. It's delicious. We try the cheddar, which is sharp, flaky, and dense. I don't enjoy the smoked cheddar, because I can't get past the smoky taste. But I adore the fetas—salty, curdy, and intense.

These are so different from the industrialized cheeses of my youth, which the writer Harold McGee calls a "simplified food that could be and is made anywhere, and that tastes of nowhere in particular." Redwood Hill's cheeses are distinctly from here—from goats that graze on the ground I'm standing on, whose diet consists largely of native thistles and scrub.

When we're done, David walks us toward the door that leads back into the creamery. He has kindly offered to show us the farm; and as much as I enjoy the creamery, the truth is, I can't wait to meet the goats.

I trail his truck along the freeway and then west for a few miles down a long, winding road hedged with tangles of blackberry bushes. Everywhere are meadows filled with brilliant yellow sorrel. In the unique ecology of this place, I see olive trees growing next to a redwood grove, which is just over the hill from a copse of palms.

It's a bright, clear spring day. We've finally had rain this month, and the land is grateful. But after several years of drought, the ground is perpetually thirsty. The rain is welcome, but much more is needed. I'm glad for a break in the weather, though, because I don't like wading through mud.

I park, and walk a short way on a gravel road toward the first shed. I smell the goats' animal scent before I see them. The yearlings are in the first pen—black, white, brown, and all combinations thereof. I walk up to the fence as they poke their heads through, crowding each other to get a sniff of my hand. The yearlings and the younger kids, whose horns have already been removed, are kept separate from the older goats, which are moved into the main barn when they turn 18 months old.

The farm keeps four primary breeds of goats: Alpines, Saanens, LaManchas, and Nubians. The first things I notice are their horizontal pupils, which I later learn increase their ability to see peripherally. Then I notice their ears, which are all so different. The Alpines' stick straight up, while the Saanens' stick out sideways. The LaManchas' are stubby and curlicue-shaped; while the Nubians, with their long, floppy ears and Roman noses, look like an entirely different species. One Nubian with a fierce overbite reminds me of Jerry Lewis in *The Nutty Professor.*

I put my hand through the fence and instantly feel a few sets of mouths gumming my fingers. Then I feel a tug on my left side and notice an Alpine chewing on my pocket while another starts gnawing on my jacket button.

I ask Trinity Smith, the farm manager, how these breeds differ in personality.

"Of the breeds that we have, the Alpines are the queens. They are dominant and aggressive and rule the roost. If there's a fight, you can pretty much bet an Alpine is involved.

"The Saanens are the large, lumbering workhorses. They love making milk and do it well, while having the sweetest, most teddy-bear-like personalities. Nubians are the softies. They are always looking for a shoulder to lean on and need reassurance before embarking on any adventure. You constantly have to hold their hoof and pat their back; but once they trust you, they become the most caring and loving of all."

"And the LaManchas?" I ask.

"They are the most high and mighty. They will love you on their terms, not yours, and in their own good time," Trinity says. "They are also the most mischievous of the lot. Any gate that's opened, fence that's jumped, or wire that's chewed, you can bet a LaMancha is responsible, grinning all the while."

As if to prove that point, a LaMancha named Calamity Jane is busy trying to open the gate with her hoof.

We move on from the yearlings and past the milking shed, where I see an elliptical platform, known as a stanchion, equipped with milking hoses. Smith tells me that the goats come here to be milked twice a day.

I hear soft, tiny bleats in the distance, the sound of hungry goat kids waiting to be fed. We walk through the barn. Trinity picks up a big plastic bucket with ten nipples on the outside. She fills the bucket with rich goat milk and opens the pen.

They come running—dozens of baby kids, all less than two days old. They are the size of small dogs, each weighing between four and six pounds. They have names like Rayna, Coquette, and Estelle and come in various combinations of white, black, cream, and brown. The larger ones push their way through the throng and start sucking on the bucket's nipples. Smith occasionally has to help a goat latch on to get good suction.

"Watch this," she says. She begins petting one of the kids on his back as he sucks from the pail. His tiny tail begins to move, wagging back and forth at warp speed.

"Do they all do that?" I ask.

She motions for me to test it out on another kid. I pick a white-and-black one and start scratching her back. Her tail wags frantically. I scratch all the kids around the bucket and their tails move back and forth like some tiny caprine chorus line.

I feel a knock against the back of my leg. I turn around; and a kid is butting me insistently, wanting to get my attention. I pick him up and nuzzle him under my neck. He bleats softly, nestles in, and starts gumming my earlobe. I sigh. I am madly in love.

I ask Smith to tell me more about the goats. "They are so faithful," she says. "They're there whenever I need a shoulder to lean on. They give their full attention. They love you. They get mad at you. And eventually they forgive you."

I could learn a lot from them, I think, as I reluctantly detach the tiny goat kid from my earlobe.

• • •

A few hours later, I'm home in our kitchen. Before I left that morning, I set out some Redwood Hill cheeses I'd bought a few days earlier from The Cheese Board, Berkeley's famed cheese collective. I put the cheeses out because I knew I'd want to try them again after my visit.

I cut myself a wedge of the Crottin, which I enjoy but am not captivated by. The Bucheret is a different story. The fat content combined with its buttery thyme flavor is enchanting. I cut a wedge, remove the rind, and take a bite. The cheese is earthy, and I can taste the thistle and scrub in the goats' milk.

I cut another wedge—creamy and lovely. I eat it, and then I cut yet one more. I know so much about this cheese now: who makes it, what fed the goats whose milk turned into it, and just how irresistible those goats are. But so far all this knowledge isn't helping me master my craving.

And so I take another bite.

Warm Goat Cheese Salad with Peaches and Honey

Serves 4

4 rounds fresh goat cheese, 1 inch thick (about 5 ounces)
½ cup bread crumbs or ½ cup toasted walnuts ground in a
    food processor to bread-crumb size
10 ounces fresh mixed salad greens, rinsed and dried
2 large peaches, pitted and sliced into 12 wedges each
4 teaspoons good-quality honey

Vinaigrette:
¼ cup good-quality extra virgin olive oil
2 tablespoons red wine vinegar
1½ teaspoons minced garlic or shallot
Salt and pepper to taste

Preheat oven to 375°F. Dip the rounds of cheese in the
bread crumbs or walnuts, making sure coating is even.

Place rounds on a baking sheet lined with parchment
paper and bake until golden, about 10 minutes.

Whisk vinaigrette ingredients together in small bowl.
Pour vinaigrette over salad greens and mix.

Place salad on plates. Place a cheese round on top of
each, and arrange peach slices around it. Drizzle cheese
with a little bit of honey.

Chapter 3

CHOCOLATE

"Satan wears many guises," warns the young priest in the movie *Chocolat*. His sermon is delivered during Lent in a small-town church in the French countryside. He offers these cautionary words at the urging of the town's repressed mayor. Evil has arrived in their village in the form of a single mother who has opened a den of iniquity—a fine chocolate shop.

"At times, Satan is the singer of a lurid song you hear on the radio," the priest continues. "At times, the author of a salacious novel. At times, the quiet man lurking in the schoolyard, asking your children if he might join their game.

"And at times," he concludes, "the maker of sweet things, mere trifles. For what could seem more harmless, more innocent, than chocolate?"

• • •

I don't think chocolate is evil—in fact, I adore it. And I eat it, like many of the foods I love, too often.

"Today we'll make pomegranate bonbons," says Malena Lopez-Maggi of The Xocolate Bar in Berkeley. Her shop has the look of a small Parisian café. The walls are painted cherry red, the ceiling is butter yellow, and the molding is a burnished gold. Crimson velvet and taffeta curtains cover the windows. Opulent chandeliers hang from the ceiling. The shop is owned by Malena and her business and romantic partner, Clive Brown, both musicians and artists (she a metalsmith, he a glass fuser).

A glass case displays fetching bonbons: apricot marzipan; Aztec, filled with cinnamon, orange, and chili; dulce de leche; gianduja, filled with hazelnut paste; lavender caramel; tamarind mango; and my favorite, fleur de sel, chocolate-covered caramel sprinkled with salt.

As Malena leads me into her tiny kitchen, I pass by a wall display of shimmering chocolates—butterflies and dragons painted with a wash of iridescent edible paint. I also see several erotic figurines—a lovely, rotund Venus of Willendorf, male torsos, and a pert set of buttocks.

Now those would make a lovely mouthful, I think as I roll up my sleeves and get down to work.

• • •

Theobroma cacao, commonly known as cacao, is a fussy plant. It grows only in the tropical regions within 20 degrees south and north of the equator, and it grows best from about 1,300 to 2,700 feet above sea level. Then it takes seven years for a cacao seedling to produce pods, which must be cut by hand with a machete. Between pod and finished product, there are many more steps—from processing the beans to conching (a process that smoothes the chocolate), tempering (a method of heating and cooling that gives it a glossy finish), and finally molding the chocolate.

Perhaps we are willing to put so much effort into producing chocolate not only because it's delicious but also because it's a drug: it contains theobromine, a chemical that functions as a stimulant, and phenylethylamine, one that targets opiate receptors in the brain. No wonder I adore it.

I sit down at a metal worktable in Malena's kitchen as she tempers the chocolate, a blend of couverture—chocolate with a high percentage of cocoa butter—from Ghana, Madagascar, and Venezuela. She heats it, then cools it, testing it for proper viscosity.

This chocolate bears little resemblance to the candy of my youth, which I also loved but for different reasons. Chocolate then meant one thing only—Halloween. I walked miles to get those sweet rewards wrapped in shiny packages on the most magical night of the year.

• • •

I'm 13 years old, and for Halloween my best friend, Pammy, and I are dressed as Bonnie and Clyde. This is our third year as the outlaws, and just once I'd like to be Bonnie. But Pammy is adamant. The boy is taller than the girl. I'm taller than Pammy. Therefore, I'm Clyde. Again.

I'm wearing pants and my father's old shirt, vest, and fedora. Pammy is in a dress, fishnet tights, and a beret. We both carry toy Derringers, and our bicycles are our getaway cars. I'm deeply attached to my purple metallic Schwinn with the sparkling silver banana seat.

We park our bikes, walk up to the first front door, and yell, "Trick or treat!" The lady who answers smiles and gives us each a miniature candy bar. We do this house after house, street after street. It's chilly, and we can see our breath in the night air. Pammy and I ride on. By the end of the evening, we have visited dozens of houses.

When I get home, I dump my stash on the table. I have more than 100 pieces of candy—Three Musketeers, Almond Joy, Nestlé Crunch, Hershey's Kiss, Kit Kat, Mounds, Butterfinger, Zagnut, Reese's, and more.

I gorge on dozens of pieces of candy, eating my least favorite first and hoarding my favorites for later. Then I climb into bed with a lump in my stomach. Before I go to sleep, I have one more piece.

• • •

Most candy doesn't excite me anymore. It's too sweet. These days I like my chocolate with some nuance. Xocolate's pomegranate bonbons fit this bill—the filling is a ganache made with a sour pomegranate juice, which balances out the sweetness of the chocolate.

My job is to decorate the bonbons. Malena hands me a pair of scissors and shows me how to cut squares from a transfer sheet made of cocoa butter. The sheet comes ready-made with an ornate burgundy floral design, and I'm supposed to place one square in the bottom of each bonbon mold. There are 20 or so per tray. Later, when the bonbons are done and turned over, the floral pattern will be on top.

I find this work that requires attention to detail tedious and annoying. When I'm done, Malena takes the tempered chocolate and floods the prepared molds. She removes the excess with a spatula and knocks the tray hard on the counter to release air bubbles. Then she pours the chocolate out so that just a chocolate shell remains.

I watch as she begins filling the molds by squirting the ganache into each square with a thin pastry tube. She asks me if I'd like to try. I take the tube and start squirting with reckless abandon. The ganache spills over the top and onto the counter.

Oops. Malena's a good sport; she scoops up the errant ganache and tells me to try again. I do, and find calibrating the squirts difficult. My impatience is winning out.

Finally, after several more miscalculated attempts, I get it more or less right. I fill up a few trays of bonbons, which Malena then sets aside to harden overnight.

"Would you like to try something else?" Malena asks as we take a brief break.

"Always," I reply.

She takes out a 100 percent cocoa bar. The percentage of cocoa refers to the total percent of cocoa butter and beans in a bar. A higher percent doesn't necessarily mean a better bar. Good chocolate is a combination of both good ingredients and good manufacturing. But I have never tried a 100 percent bar, and I'm curious.

She hands me a piece. I rub it and smell the bitter aroma. I taste it, and my mouth instantly puckers. The bar is incredibly astringent and my mouth goes completely dry. I couldn't make this chocolate a habit.

But despite my visceral reaction, I find it captivating— it's like eating a slice of Earth.

• • •

Scott and I are taking Matthew and Jack trick-or-treating around our neighborhood. Jack is dressed as

Indiana Jones, and Matthew is a ninja. I'm a witch, as I have been every year for Halloween since the boys were born. I'm wearing a floor-length, midnight-blue opera cape with a hood, which covers up my jeans, high-top sneakers, and sweatshirt. In honor of the occasion, I wear a brilliant rhinestone brooch, designed in the 1950s by one of my great-uncles, Henry Bogoff. My eyes are rimmed with iridescent, emerald-green shadow; and my lips are painted crimson red.

We walk downhill to a street near our home. This particular street takes Halloween seriously. It's closed to traffic, and each house is more wonderful than the last. One house displays carved jack-o'-lanterns so beautiful they should be in a gallery. Another family has lined their driveway with smoky cauldrons, leading visitors to the garage, where they are showing the horror-movie classic *Nosferatu* on a giant white sheet. The house next door has a graveyard with tombstones of dead financial institutions such as Lehman Brothers. Welcome to Halloween in Berkeley!

Ghosts, goblins, bats, vampires, fairies, elves, imps, wizards, and a troll flit by. Eerie violin music wafts softly from one yard. An occasional wolf's howl pierces the night sky. We keep walking, and the boys' bags eventually fill up with candy.

We walk until our feet ache. When we get home, the boys pour their loot out on our dining-room table. "How much can we eat?" they ask, practically panting with eagerness. I've tried rationing their candy in the past, and they've pestered me so much that this time, I decide to let them gorge. "As much as you want," I say.

Has their mother gone mad? They cannot believe their good fortune!

They start piling their candy into groups of most favorite, medium favorite, and least favorite. It must run in the bloodline. But unlike me, they go for their favorites first.

• • •

Though Halloween has in recent years become a sugar orgy, chocolate, in all its original dark glory, is still mysterious. It is, in its own way, a bridge between worlds—a kind of accessible magic. It is a magic I experience most when imbibing my favorite cacao indulgence—sipping chocolate.

Sipping chocolate is not the same as hot chocolate. It contains no milk or added sugar. It is usually made from just two ingredients, chocolate and water—though I prefer it with a pinch of chili powder.

Malena uses a mixture of different kinds of couverture, which gives the sipping chocolate a creaminess that is impossible to duplicate at home with cocoa powder. She uses a couverture from Venezuela, which has some berry undertones, mixed with one from Madagascar, which adds sharpness and tang.

She stirs the chocolate and water together on the stove. I peer into the pot. It's dark, shiny, and lusciously creamy.

Malena pours some into a cup for me, then pours the rest into her sipping-chocolate machine, a glass container rimmed with copper. Inside, the mixing paddles continuously stir the chocolate. I take a sip. The drink is simple and delicious. It's liquid velvet—full of fruit, citrus, earth, and sun.

"I'm undone," I say to Malena, who smiles, knowing that I'm echoing the words Johnny Depp's character utters in Chocolat.

• • •

My mother stands over the stove, stirring together My-T-Fine pudding mix and milk in a pan. I'm 13. She makes only one chocolate dessert, and this is it. I peer into the pot and watch as the mixture bubbles and thickens. She pours it into four glass bowls and puts them into the refrigerator to cool.

A few hours later, I take out a bowl of pudding and dig in. The top layer has hardened, forming a skin, which I remove with my spoon; I don't like the rubbery consistency. The prize is underneath—a velvety, creamy pudding, satisfying in its sweetness.

My mother wears her dislike of cooking as a badge of honor, a symbol, perhaps, of her ambivalence about being a wife and a mother. The adventurer in her would rather be traveling the world with only a backpack. But like many women of her generation, she clung to her safer, suburban self by getting married and having children.

One day, when I'm 17, I'm mystified but delighted when my mother asks me if I'd like to join her in making a chocolate flan. Not My-T-Fine pudding, but the real thing.

She melts sugar in a pan; and our kitchen fills with a sweet, merry scent. When all the sugar has melted, she takes out a green-and-white, plastic, fluted mold with a removable bottom and places it on the counter. Then she pours the liquid sugar into the mold.

Meanwhile, I whisk together evaporated milk, melted chocolate, vanilla, and eggs and pour the custard into the mold, over the hardening sugar. I feel awkward standing next to my mother in a kitchen. Cooking is not a language we share. She doesn't enjoy it, and I don't yet know it.

We're making a nonbaked flan, which will set as it cools in the refrigerator. But when my mother tries to move the mold, it doesn't cooperate. "That's odd," she says, and gives it another tug. It still doesn't budge. "Give me a hand here, will you?"

I walk over to the counter and start tugging on the mold, too. It still doesn't move. I grab it more firmly and try to jiggle it free. "It's stuck to the counter," I tell her.

Working together, we yank the mold hard. Suddenly it breaks. The removable bottom stays fused to the countertop while the bowl flies off in our hands. Flan dribbles, and then cascades, out of the mold, onto the countertop and the floor, until nothing is left but the fused bottom filled with now-hardened sugar.

"It's the plastic," I say. "The mold is made of goddamn plastic."

We begin to laugh. "We're imbeciles," my mother croaks.

"Absolute morons!" I scream.

We laugh so hard our eyes water.

• • •

As I get ready to leave Malena's shop, I notice a display of bars from several fine chocolatiers: Amedei, Domori, and Michel Cluizel. Sitting in the middle is a bar called Mo's Bacon Bar made by the Chicago chocolatier Katrina Markoff of Vosges Chocolate. The beautiful white packaging shows a piece of crisp bacon curved invitingly toward a piece of chocolate, as if they're getting ready to embrace.

Bacon chocolate? How? And why?

I turn the package over. On the back is a note from Markoff: "Really," she writes, "what doesn't taste better with bacon?"

Maybe. But I'm dubious. Bacon is a perfect food in its own right, as is chocolate. What could they possibly offer each other?

I unwrap the bar and follow the package's over-the-top instructions to engage all my senses. I rub my fingers over the chocolate; and as I do, the wonderful scent of bacon fills the air.

I put a small piece in my mouth. As the smoky bacon melds with the slightly sweet chocolate, I break out into a huge grin. It's strange and fabulous. Such audacity! I don't know what I love more: the taste of the bar or the inventiveness of the entire enterprise. I start to laugh and can't stop: two of my food obsessions—pork and chocolate—in one complicated bite.

• • •

A few months after I make chocolate with Malena, my family and I take a vacation to Gualala, a coastal town about three and a half hours north of San Francisco.

I have a bar of bacon chocolate with me. A vacation is a time to indulge in odd pleasures, and I know the right moment to eat it will present itself, which it soon does.

Our favorite restaurant in town is the Bones Roadhouse, a first-rate BBQ joint with a fine selection of meats and microbrews. It occurs to me that the owner, Mike Thomas, who goes by the nickname Bone Daddy, just might appreciate the bacon chocolate. After all, there is nothing this man can't do with a side of hog.

And, really, what doesn't taste better with bacon, as the package says?

When we arrive, Santana's "Black Magic Woman" is playing on the stereo. Biker paraphernalia hang on the walls and ceiling, including miniature toy choppers, license plates, and a Harley-Davidson garage sign. A skeleton sits grinning on a Radio Flyer that has been turned into a chopper. And, as an homage to the wild Pacific just outside, a rubber shark with an amputated leg in its mouth is mounted over the back door.

Bone Daddy comes out to say hello. He's a big, burly man, well over six feet tall, with a graying ponytail, kind blue-green eyes, and a faded orange Harley-Davidson T-shirt.

"Bone Daddy, I brought you a gift," I say and hand him the chocolate bar.

He breaks off a piece and pops it in his mouth. After a moment he smiles just as I did. "What a trip." He waits a minute and then, like a connoisseur tasting a fine wine, says, "If you give it time, the chocolate and bacon flavors merge. I like it."

We're sitting at a table near the bar. Sunlight streams in as we look out the restaurant's window at the seemingly endless Pacific Ocean. A waitress comes by. "Bacon chocolate?" she says doubtfully.

"Try it," I offer. "You never know." She does, and pronounces it weird. A busboy sporting a greased-back ponytail stops by. "Try some," I suggest. He does and seems baffled. Another waitress comes by, tries it, and smiles.

As I drive the winding road back to our rental house, I think how powerful chocolate is. In *Chocolat*, it even has the power to change lives: the single-mom chocolate-shop proprietress sets down roots in the town and finds love, her friend finds the strength to leave her abusive husband, and the mayor realizes his marriage is dead and takes a chance on a new relationship.

I'm looking to change my life, too. But apparently chocolate isn't going to be my catalyst. There's one last food obsession for me to explore. It's too late to turn back—and I wouldn't want to anyway.

• • •

Sipping Chocolate
with Cinnamon and Chili

Serves 6

2 cups water (use distilled if you don't like the taste of
   your tap water)
2 cups (about 8 ounces) chocolate couverture buttons
   (E. Guittard 61% and 72% are great choices; you can
   also substitute any good-quality eating chocolate, but not
   cocoa powder or chocolate chips, because they do not
   have enough cocoa butter)
Pinch of ground Mexican cinnamon and/or Kashmiri chili
   for each serving

Bring water to a boil. Turn off heat and add chocolate.
Let mixture sit 1 minute, then whisk until smooth.

Serve in demitasse cups. Sprinkle cinnamon and/or chili
over each serving, if desired.

Recipe courtesy of Malena Lopez-Maggi.

Chapter 4

OLIVES

Rarely have I met an olive I didn't like, or at least respect. I love everything about them: their delicious vitamin-filled flesh, their sensual oval shape, the astonishing variety. They are the king of my cravings. And, as such, they do not last the night in our refrigerator.

So here I am, heading north on Highway 101 to McEvoy Ranch, an organic olive grower and producer in Petaluma—once more hoping for liberation through knowledge.

I turn off the freeway onto a rural road and head west toward the ranch. Though the directions are complicated, I reach my destination. Since moving to California more than 20 years ago, I rarely get lost.

My sense of direction was not always so finely tuned. I grew up in Rockland County, New York, yet all through my youth and long after I left, I couldn't tell you that I lived a half hour north of New York City, or west of the Hudson River, for that matter. I had some kind of geographical amnesia. Here, though, in California, north of my home are vineyards, east past the hills lies the Sacramento Valley, and west is the Pacific Ocean.

I drive past iris-dappled ridges. Cows amble slowly through a field. I cross a stone bridge and then pass an old white-clapboard one-room schoolhouse. Further on, by a giant cypress tree, I see the small sign for McEvoy Ranch and turn down a rough, unpaved road, which has me bouncing in my seat.

The ranch's cast-iron gate is topped by a figure of a giant bronze hare with enormous ears stretching toward the sky. With an inscrutable expression, he looks like he has stepped from the pages of *Alice in Wonderland*. The gate slides open.

Ahead are several California-ranch-style buildings surrounded by pots of rosemary and climbing vines. Birds are singing; and as far as I can see, are rolling hills filled with olive groves. I park the car and get out, amused that, after a lifetime of consuming olives, I know so little about them. Only the other day I learned that black olives are simply green olives allowed to ripen.

• • •

When Nan Tucker McEvoy, granddaughter of Michael de Young, founder of the *San Francisco Chronicle* and San Francisco's de Young Museum, bought the ranch back in 1991, its 550 acres were zoned for agriculture. The wine industry was well established in Sonoma and the nearby Napa Valley, but few people in the region were growing olives, and none on a large scale. Nan could have bought a few goats, declared her land used for agriculture, kicked back, and called it a day. Instead, she planted olive groves.

Nan was interested in producing Tuscan-style olive oil, which has a green, fruity, and peppery flavor profile. She hired experts to amend the soil, which had been sorely depleted during its previous service as a dairy farm, and worked with a Tuscan agronomist who picked the varietals to plant. To start, 3,000 trees were shipped over from Italy. Today, the ranch is fully planted and counts more than 18,000 trees in 14 orchards, planted by cultivar, or varietal. It is the largest producer of organic estate olive oil in the country.

The ranch grows six main varietals: Frantoios, Leccinos, Pendolinos, Coratinas, Leccio del Cornos, and Maurinos, all of which have different tastes and attributes.

These six are only a few of the thousands of varieties of olives grown. But it wasn't until I was 23 that I realized olives weren't simply black or green and canned. I learned this by chance while wandering through the streets of a medieval city.

• • •

I'm in Fribourg, a Swiss city not far from the French border. I'm living with my boyfriend, whom I'll call Stefan, a professor at the University of Fribourg, whom I met while studying philosophy in graduate school in the States. He is a kind man with an interesting mind. My father died just a few months earlier at age 56, and I have moved to Switzerland in hope of healing my sad heart.

Stefan and I walk through the narrow cobblestone streets, past Saint Nicholas Cathedral with its Gothic spires. The air is chilly. He is taking me to the farmer's market where he buys vegetables every week. It's 1983, and I've never heard of a farmer's market, let alone visited one.

We go to different stalls. One has dozens of varieties of lettuces, and I'm smitten by a clover-shaped, bitter green known as *rampon*. We continue on our way until we see a farmer selling two dozen varieties of olives. There are green ones, black ones, brown ones, and purple ones. Some have been cured in salt and are shriveled. Others, which have been cured in liquid brine, are round and plump. All are dazzling. The vendor beckons me over and asks me if I'd like to try some. "*Oui*," I say, hesitating, "*juste un peu*." I'm overwhelmed by the selection, so I let Stefan choose.

As we walk on, I open the bag and try one. It's a meaty, salty Kalamata. After a few bites, inexplicably, I begin to cry. It was only two months earlier that my mother, who lives in Palo Alto, California, called me in New York to tell me my father was dying.

"Is he really dying?" I asked. "Yes," she said. *He's been dying my whole life*, I thought, hanging up.

I got on the plane and visited him the next day. When I walked into his hospital room, I knew that this time it was true. The whites of his eyes were yellow—a sign of liver failure. He had pneumonia, and his body was finally giving out.

This was the end of a journey that had begun three years earlier, when he had a heart transplant at Stanford University Medical Center, receiving the heart of a 20-year-old man who had died in a motorcycle accident. All was well for the first few months. Then my father's body rejected his new heart. To stop the rejection, doctors administered huge doses of steroids, which had devastating effects. He grew ape-like hair on his arms and hands. His spinal column collapsed. He had stood 6'1"; when he died, he was 5'6". The steroids had drained the fat from his limbs and pooled it in his chin and stomach. My handsome, vain father, who was so brave and fought so hard to live, ended life looking like a hirsute Humpty Dumpty.

When he saw me, he gave me a dazzling, magnificent smile. Despite all our fights, I went over to him and held him in my arms.

The next morning I came to visit. He was slipping in and out of consciousness. All day, my mother and I sat by his bedside. At one point the phone rang. It was my sister's former mother-in-law. "Dad," I said softly in his ear. "It's Naomi on the phone. Remember Mark's mother? Remember you never could stand her?"

His eyes fluttered open. "I still can't," he whispered in a hoarse voice.

Our vigil continued. I sat by his bed, holding his hand. "I love you, Dad," I said, crying. It was hard for me to utter these words, because I had yet to forgive him, but I knew I wouldn't get another chance.

"I love you," he said.

Those were the last words he ever spoke. He died the next day.

• • •

The olive trees at McEvoy Ranch are beginning to bud. It's mid-April; and in just a month's time, they'll be covered in a riot of blossoms. When the flowers fall, I'm told, the land looks like it's covered in snow.

I'm on the first orchard tour of the season. The trees have been pruned to stay low and grow wide. All of the olives here are picked young, in keeping with the Tuscan flavor profile that Nan McEvoy prefers. They are also picked by hand; and because of the ranch's specific pruning techniques, quantity is sacrificed for quality. Each tree will eventually yield 50 to 80 pounds of fruit; it takes 80 to 100 pounds of fruit to produce a gallon of oil. The fruit will not be ready to harvest until fall.

We end our tour with an olive-oil tasting. The room is bright and cheerful. I sit near an old Louis Vuitton steamer trunk, next to a Wayne Thiebaud painting of cakes.

We're given a brief description of oil's traits, both positive and negative. I savor the labels of the undesirable qualities: fusty, musty, vinegary, rancid, and winey. We hold small tasting cups of oil in our hands to warm it. I take a sniff—it smells fresh, with hints of tomatoes and arugula. I sip. It coats my mouth and slides down the back of my throat. It's a distinct oil—pungent, fruity, and bitter.

For most in my group, the main attraction is the oil. But for me, it's the olives, also called "table olives." McEvoy harvests only one acre of table olives, though this is becoming a larger enterprise.

Curing olives takes work. You have to leach the bitterness out of the olive slowly, over time. The methods used to do this include dry curing, where olives are packed in salt for several months; water curing, which involves soaking, rinsing, and resoaking many times; and curing the olives in oil or brine, either of which can take up to several months. McEvoy brine-cures its olives. The result now sits on the table before me in glass bowls.

The kitchen has set out a dozen small plates of just-picked spinach dressed with light vinaigrette made from the ranch's olive oil. I scoop out some olives, place them on top of the salad, and eat. The greens are wonderfully fresh; and the olives are small, peppery, and a little bitter. I'm not sure I like them. Like the oil, they're young. I prefer more buttery olives. But I won't discount them yet. I need to give them more time. I buy some jars to take home.

I'm rewarded for my patience. Though the young, grassy olives are not familiar, over time I've come to enjoy them. But even more, I appreciate discovering that a food I've loved so much for so long can still wear many unexpected faces.

• • •

Though I've learned a lot about harvesting and curing olives, I've yet to figure out why this food in particular has such a strong hold on me. Then, a few months after my tour of McEvoy Ranch, I meet Abbie Scianamblo.

Abbie is the founder of Sorelle Paradiso, an olive-oil and table-olive company in Tulare County, in California's Central Valley. Abbie grows Sevillano olives on 44 acres of old orchards; and her company's name, which means "The Paradiso Sisters" in Italian, pays homage to her great-grandmother Anna Paradiso and Anna's sister, Francesca, who farmed olives several generations ago in Italy. Her olives are big and green, with a creamy, soft finish.

Along with growing olives, Abbie is a certified Ayurvedic practitioner. In Ayurveda, which is the traditional Indian science of health and longevity, diet plays a large role in treatment.

When I tell her I'm baffled that olives have such a hold on me, she replies, "It's the combination of the shape, texture, and taste. The oval shape is sensually pleasing, the salt calms the nervous system, and the oily meat satiates the body. And their unctuous quality is particularly healing, especially for our lifestyle, which is dry and fast-paced—we're always running, and olives oil the system."

This makes sense. While I do love the shape, the saltiness, and the meatiness of olives, perhaps I've also been "oiling" my system all these years.

I tell Abbie it's interesting that people talk about the value of the Mediterranean diet—which is based on olive oil, whole grains, and greens—in a kind of vacuum, as if the diet is simply a distillation of specific vitamins, antioxidants, and fats. But the grains, the greens, and the olives all come from the earth first, cared for and cultivated by hard work and helped along with the grace and good will of nature.

Abbie agrees. "If people understand where their food comes from and how it grows, they become more connected to their health and to themselves.

"Every thing lives in accordance to cycles and seasons," she continues. "The more connected you are with your food sources and with your own family history, the more connected you are with yourself as a human being."

What started as a conversation about olives has turned into a conversation about life.

Abbie is right that olives are fundamentally healthy, but my relationship with them isn't. I'm not really connected to olives, any more than I am to sausage or cheese or chocolate. When I'm eating these foods, I'm obsessed and alone. And that's not enough for me anymore.

• • •

Roasted Tomato Soup
with Olives and Basil

Serves 4

6 large ripe tomatoes, chopped in half (about 3 pounds)
1 large onion, peeled and chopped into 6 wedges
¼ cup good-quality extra virgin olive oil
2 teaspoons sherry vinegar
12 green olives (Sevillanos are a good choice), pitted
   and quartered
¼ cup basil, washed and cut into chiffonades
Salt and pepper to taste

Preheat oven to 350°F. Gently toss tomatoes and onion wedges in large bowl with olive oil. On a parchment-lined baking sheet, place tomatoes and onions cut side down and drizzle with remaining olive oil from bowl. Bake until both tomatoes and onions are soft, about 45 minutes to 1 hour.

When tomatoes are cool enough to handle, remove skins and place tomatoes in medium-sized stockpot. Add onions as well as all drippings and oil remaining on baking sheet. Puree with hand blender. Add vinegar and bring to a simmer over medium-high heat. Reduce heat to low and cook until flavors have blended, about 10 minutes. Add a small amount of water if soup is too thick.

Season with salt and pepper. Serve in bowls, topped with a sprinkling of olives and basil.

Chapter 5

SQUASH

I'm driving over a bridge. I hate bridges, ever since I had a panic attack on one a few years ago. It's the same one I'm on now. But here I am, headed from my home in Berkeley toward a small coastal town about two hours north.

I'm going to cook with a meditation teacher and chef whom I'll call Eric. Eric is well known for his work combining meditation and food. "I want to cook with you," I told him, hoping he'd say yes.

"Come visit," he said. So I am.

After what seems like an eternity, I finally reach the other side.

• • •

"Excitement is not the same as pleasure."

Eric tells me this as he pours me a mug of tea before we begin to cook. He's in his 60s, portly, and balding.

"When you are excited, the object of your excitement must disappear so you can have more of it. But for something to be truly pleasurable, you must have some connection to it."

I look out the window of Eric's kitchen. It's a typical spring day in Northern California—chilly and fogged in.

His kitchen is modest, serviceable, and small. No granite countertops, Sub-Zero refrigerator, or Wolf range in sight. Being a chef and a meditation teacher probably doesn't pay much. Then again, maybe being a meditation teacher means you don't need the fancy gadgets.

I start unpacking my bag of groceries. When I called him a few days earlier to ask what I should bring, he replied, "Just bring stuff."

So I did: Chantenay carrots, Yellow Finn potatoes, purple cabbage, red chilies, navel oranges, leeks, celery root, and a winter squash—all produce from my weekly farm box, which I supplement with some lemons from my garden.

"So what are we making?" I ask.

He begins grouping the vegetables into possible dishes. The potatoes and carrots join up with the chilies, along with the leeks. The squash gets matched with the celery root. He returns the cabbage to me.

"Leek, potato, and carrot curry with coconut, over soba noodles," he says, "with a side of roasted vegetables."

He fires up his cream-colored Wedgewood oven, circa 1940. Then he picks up the celery root, a funky-looking, gnarly tuber; takes out two simple knives with wooden handles; cuts the root in half; and hands one piece to me. We begin peeling, my knife gliding almost effortlessly through the fibrous, crenellated skin. The knives, he tells me, are from Japan and are designed for vegetables. Most knives we use in the United States are meant for cutting meat.

We peel the celery root and slice it into half-moon pieces. His slices are uniform, his technique elegant—

a combination saw and slice. He scoops up the pieces and places them in a well-used, deep-orange cast-iron pan.

I notice his hands. They are small and calloused, their movements precise. There's something about the way they handle the vegetables—carefully and with respect—that I find attractive.

We are standing near one another, and I get a brief whiff of Eric's scent. Woodsy and masculine.

He holds up the squash. It's a kabocha, an unearthly-looking, blue-green giant. He gazes into my eyes and says, "Isn't this beautiful?"

He puts it on the counter and tries to cut it in half, but the squash is not as pliable as the celery root. He tips the knife forward and applies more pressure. Still nothing happens.

"We may not be eating this squash today after all," he says, grunting, as he gives the knife one more firm push. The squash finally yields.

He tells me to scoop out the seeds—and he passes me a spoon. I'm disappointed. I've always found putting my hands into squash sensual. I love the feeling of ripping the seeds as they cling to their inner chambers.

But I do not protest. As it is, I'm finding cooking with Eric a covertly sensual experience. I usually cook alone. So if ever I feel intimate, it's usually with the food, not with another person.

Maybe it's Eric's vibes. All I know is that I'm slowly getting turned on. I decide that using a spoon instead of my fingers will create the distance I need between the squash and me—and by extension, between Eric and me. Since I'm married, that's probably a good thing.

I scoop the seeds out, chamber by chamber, and put them into a bowl. "What do you do with these?" I ask him.

"Compost," he says brusquely. "Send them back to where they came from."

We peel and cut the squash into segments and add them to the pan. He pours on the olive oil and mixes the vegetables with his hands. He takes a pinch of Himalayan salt, pinkish in hue; rubs it between his fingers over the dish; and then pops the dish into the oven.

"It's time to cook the curry," he says, which is fine, except for one thing: I'm hungry. Starving, in fact. I was so nervous about driving over the bridge earlier that I barely ate breakfast, and I'm getting a little light-headed. "Eric," I say, "do you have anything I can eat now?"

"Of course," he says. I am grateful to him for answering my need directly, instead of asking me to examine the nature of my hunger or suggesting I practice delayed gratification.

"How about an egg?" he asks. I nod yes. He puts some butter into a small pan; and when it starts to sizzle, he cracks the egg open. It's huge, with an orange-yellow yolk.

He cooks it on one side, then flips it, cooks it some more, and serves it. The yolk is runny, which I don't like. But I don't want to seem ungrateful or picky, so I eat it. It's fresh and tastes a little like just-mown grass.

I find it interesting that along with being a cook and a teacher, Eric is also something of a mother—a quality I find appealing.

But I'm still hungry.

Eric sees the look on my face and asks me if I want more food. I nod yes again. He makes me some sourdough toast, dense with walnuts. I eat half and leave the rest. I feel virtuous. I'm not eating the whole thing. I'm satisfied—my gluttony, for the moment at least, is at bay.

"Would you like some olives?" he asks.

Could he have known?

He opens the refrigerator and says, "Oops, there's only one left in the jar."

Who leaves one olive in a jar? Who has that kind of discipline? Yet since one olive is all he has, one is all I eat.

• • •

A week earlier, I'd sat in a concrete auditorium with 100 other people and heard a lecture by Eric titled "The Ceremony of Eating Just One Corn Chip."

I sometimes find mindfulness practices with regard to food forced, even tedious. But since eating only one of anything is difficult for me, I'm game.

Eric begins his talk by asking what it means to be awake. "It means having your own experience," he says. "Not mine. Yours. See with your own eyes. Hear with your own ears. Smell with your own nose. Taste with your own tongue.

"Most of us would rather be right than have our own experience. What *should* I be tasting, rather than what *am* I tasting?

"Before we eat our chip," he says, "let's say a prayer."

He holds up his chip, then gets sidetracked. "There are many ways to eat this," he says. "You can nibble. You can pop it in your mouth. But however you eat it, notice it. Observe it. Smell it. Touch it. Use all your senses."

I touch mine. It feels rough, like sandpaper. I smell it and don't get much of anything.

"In America," he continues, "it seems that happiness means not having to relate to anything. You can consume without having to relate. It passes through us, and we wonder why we're not nourished."

Then he pops his chip into his mouth.

"But the prayer!" the audience howls. "What about the prayer?"

"Oh, right," he laughs, "the prayer."

We bow our heads, looking into our Dixie cups, each holding a single chip.

"May your eating of this corn chip be of benefit to all beings. May all beings be free from suffering."

I hear the sounds of 100 people crunching. Most finish quickly. A few stalwarts nibble delicately, intently.

"What do you think?" Eric asks.

"Do you have more?" someone retorts.

People start to laugh.

"The oil is rancid," says another.

I taste mine. She's right—the oil is off. This chip isn't doing it for me.

"What do you think, Eric?" someone from the audience asks.

"Salt, grease, tasteless pulp in my mouth," he says, koan-like. "I can never eat enough corn chips to be satisfied because there's no there there. And if I wasn't paying attention, I'd keep eating them to try to get what isn't there.

"Compare this to an orange," he says, "which is sweet and tastes like sunshine. When you taste something, don't only let your mouth respond. Let your heart respond. There's a lot of food in this world that doesn't have much to offer your heart."

• • •

I stare at the carrots on Eric's counter. They are bright orange and chubby, vibrant and full of life. My heart responds.

He picks up a leek, a vegetable that has always confounded me. "How far up the stalk can you eat?" I ask him.

"Try it," he says.

So I do. As I make my way up the stalk, nibble by nibble, I notice there actually is a point where it becomes inedible. I have my answer.

He slices through the leeks lengthwise and rinses the dirt from between their layers. He cuts them, as he does most vegetables, on the diagonal, which allows more surface area to cook.

He puts the leeks in a pan with some ghee.

"Why ghee?" I ask. He explains that clarified butter allows you to cook vegetables over a higher temperature without burning them. This keeps the flavors intact and sharp.

He puts more ghee into a separate pan, heats it, then adds the sliced carrots and potatoes. They hit the pan with a resounding sizzle. The ghee's nutty, toasty scent wafts past my nose.

We begin making the curry spice. Eric grabs some cumin, clove, turmeric, cardamom, and cinnamon sticks. He throws in some mustard seeds for good measure. He grinds the spices in an electric grinder and puts them into a bowl. Then he holds the mixture up to my nose. "What do you smell?" he asks.

I take a deep sniff. "Cumin," I reply.

"Right," he says. "When you are making curry, no one spice should dominate. So we will endeavor to balance the spices out."

Endeavor is such an oddly formal word. Something about it bugs me.

"Yes," I say, unable to suppress my rising sarcasm. "Let's *endeavor* to do so."

Why am I getting angry?

The odd formality of his word seems dissonant with the rising intimacy I feel cooking next to him. I realize, to my chagrin, that I want him to flirt with me; and I want to flirt back. And the word *endeavor* suddenly feels like a rejection.

The skin on the back of my neck begins to prickle and feel flushed. I try to ignore it and concentrate on the task at hand.

He adds more clove, cardamom, and cinnamon— the sweeter spices, to add balance.

He holds the bowl up to my nose and tells me to smell again. The cumin has receded, and the other spices now register. The mix is more balanced.

"Your endeavor has been successful," I murmur.

He looks up. He's quiet for a moment, and then says, "Let's grate the ginger." He uses a special grater that minces the ginger so finely that it gives up its juice. He has the practiced hands of a chef. *Hands need to be useful,* I think as I watch him. *Hands are lonely if they're not.*

I wonder about cooking and loneliness. I know that Eric lost his mother when he was three. I can't imagine a greater loss or greater sorrow. As a mother of two boys, I can't fathom not being in their lives. If I were gone, it would blow their world to pieces. My mother is still alive; and the idea of losing her, even now, unmoors me.

After Eric mixes in the curry spices, coconut milk, and a dash of vermouth, we taste the sauce. I tell him it needs more salt and he tells me it doesn't. "Sometimes when you think you need salt, what you really need is brightness," he says, squeezing some lemon into the dish. I taste the sauce again. He's right.

I hesitate to ask my next question, but something urges me on.

"Eric," I say gently, "do you think your decision to devote your life to food has something to do with losing your mother so young?"

He's silent. He turns his back to me. He stands in front of the stove for a good half minute. Then I hear it—a sharp intake of breath, followed by a sob. "Excuse me," he says as he leaves the room.

Perhaps I shouldn't have asked this. But it's an honest question. Somewhere in the tangle of mothering and food is a key to my eating, and I want to know his answer—for my own sake.

I don't know whether to stay in his kitchen or go find him. Since I can't decide, I make myself useful and begin cleaning up. A few minutes later he reemerges, his eyes rimmed in red. "Let's eat," he says.

• • •

We decide to eat outside. It's a little chilly, but I like the way the air feels on my face and skin. I put down place mats, plates, silverware, and napkins. He serves our meal on several platters. One of them, a deep, sapphire blue that he has glued back together, has a jagged crack down the center.

We sit at the small, round wooden table. I see some peony shoots poking up through the ground. I adore peonies. They are beautiful and complex—what seems like a thousand petals folding over another thousand.

I'm sure Eric wants to say a blessing. He's a Buddhist, after all; and from my limited experience, when you eat with a Buddhist, there's usually a prayer involved. I bow my head. Silence. I wait. More silence. *A silent prayer?* I wonder. *Is he waiting for me? Is he angry with me for asking about his mother?*

I don't know any Buddhist prayers by heart, but I could make one up; they usually involve a phrase like "May all beings be blessed." I could share the prayers I say when I light Sabbath candles with my family on Friday nights. I'm sure Eric would find this acceptable. What I don't quite understand is why this sudden silence threatens to bring out my inner Henny Youngman. If he doesn't say something soon, I'm going to break into a Borscht Belt routine.

"Eric," I finally gasp, "you're the Buddhist. *Say* something." I'm so relieved when he finally begins to speak that I don't hear what he says, except the phrase "May all beings be blessed."

He serves our food. I attempt to eat slowly, not because it comes naturally, but because I think I should.

We talk. This time he asks me about my family. I say a little bit about my always-thin sister, who has survived 50-plus years largely on pretzels; and about my reedy mother, a former model, who takes pride in her indifference to food. The conversation veers toward beauty and body image, which I'd find fascinating if I weren't feeling so vulnerable. Whatever our age or our size, we want to know we are beautiful to someone; and I find myself wanting to be beautiful to him.

Eric tells me the story of how he lost 25 pounds by living the Julia Child diet of no second portions. He lost a quarter of a pound a week; and after two years, he was 25 pounds thinner. I'm amazed at his patience. He goes on to tell me that after he broke up with his longtime girlfriend, he gained back all the weight and then some.

"I lose weight when I'm heartbroken," I say. I tell him that the only time my sister said my body was beautiful was when I was 20. I was so distraught over a breakup that I couldn't keep food down and managed to whittle myself down to a size 6.

We talk some more. I eat more of the celery root and the curry. After a while, we stop.

Eric's plate is clean. Mine still has some food left on it. He scrapes my leftovers into the compost bin. I clear the table as he cleans the kitchen.

When we're finished cleaning up, I thank him and begin gathering my things. Before I leave, he asks if I would like to have a quick cup of tea. I say I have to be hitting the road, but something in his eyes stops me. He seems lonely. He pours me a cup from a flask. I taste something odd. He sees my puzzled face and says, "Vanilla ice cream."

He puts vanilla ice cream in his tea?

Without my asking my question out loud, he answers, "Because I like it.

"So," he says casually, watching me pack up my tape recorder, notebook, and pens, "your husband probably has a regular job, right?"

A flush of heat travels up my spine and into my face. My husband? What does it matter what my husband does? And why do the words "regular job" seem suspect—as if he's suggesting that my husband is some kind of genial grunt?

Now it's my turn to become formal, to put some distance between us. "My husband," I begin, "is a writer and editor. He—"

I don't finish my sentence because Eric has picked up my hand, tracing his finger over mine. "You're a wood type," he says, referring to traditional Chinese medicine's theory of type constitution. I laugh without meaning to, thinking his words are as awkward as if he'd asked me to see his etchings. Then I look up and see his eyes—sad, watchful, and compelling.

These are the kinds of moments that can decide the fate of a marriage. Do I continue to let him touch my finger? Do I take that step into an unknown sea?

I let his hand linger on mine for just a moment, then withdraw. I don't say anything. We finish our tea in silence. I thank him and leave.

• • •

That night, I lie in bed, trying to ignore the image of his face that keeps appearing in my mind. I imagine his fingers on my cheek and feel the skin on my chest flush.

I wonder why I'm feeling this way. I love my husband. Little in my dating history would suggest that I would meet someone whom I'd share my life with intimately and happily for decades. But I was fortunate enough to do just that.

So I rarely have crushes. Eric is dumpy and middle-aged—but then again, so am I. He's smart and articulate, but I know a lot of smart and articulate people.

Then I figure it out. It's the quality of his attention that attracts me: direct and present. Eric is sad when he's sad, happy when he's happy, and annoyed when he's annoyed. After 40 years of practice, he shows up. And that draws me to him.

I'm surprised. Surprised that I can't stop thinking about him but, even more, surprised by this knot of sadness sitting right in the middle of my chest.

• • •

A few days later, Eric sends me an e-mail.

He tells me that as a follow-up, he wants to offer me some advice.

"What I noticed is that you left food on your plate and food in the bowls and pans. What you might consider is a practice of 'leaving no trace,' cleaning your plate and cleaning the bowls and pans. Wasting food outside the body is closely associated with wasting food inside the body. Value food, even small amounts. To value food is to value yourself, your thoughts, your feelings, everything."

Hold on. I thought that by *not* eating everything on my plate, I had done the right thing. I wasn't hungry, so I didn't eat. Whatever happened to "Eat when you're hungry, and stop when you're satisfied"? I feel reprimanded, like a poor student.

We begin an e-mail correspondence. I ask him why I should clean my plate of food if I'm no longer hungry. He writes that I asked for toast and had one bite. "What was that about? Don't have it on your plate. Clean out the pots and bowls. It's a 'practice'—and if you do not wish to undertake it, fine, make up some excuse why it's impractical, and get on with your life."

I feel myself getting angrier. Is this the Buddhist version of telling me to fuck off? Who the hell does he think he is?

I sit with it for a few more days. I drag out my zafu, which has been gathering dust on the top of my linen closet. I've never been much of a meditator—yoga is my main spiritual practice. But this anger is sitting squarely on my chest, and I'm not sure how to release it except to sit with it.

The longer I sit, the softer my anger becomes, giving way, instead, to grief. Grief for all those times I've tried to eat through loneliness, through the sadness of life; grief for my aging body. The initial titillation of flirting and being flirted with has given way to something else, something deeper.

We speak the next day. "The thing is, Dayna, that you need to take care of food and not discard it. Things in the bowl, things on the plate, things in the pot. Start taking care of food inside and outside. Start valuing it. See what happens."

As I hang up the phone, I think about Eric's words and realize that my whole drama with him, the flirting and the yearning, is a sideshow, a distraction. He's interesting, but it's my relationship with food that needs my attention. I could say no to Eric, but I still can't say no to some foods.

But I also realize something else. Eric had upbraided me for not finishing my meal. And he had a point about leftovers. On the other hand, the food I ate that day satisfied me: I didn't stuff myself. I stopped when I'd had enough. And I'd done it without any of the seductive foods—beyond that lone olive.

• • •

Curried Potatoes and Carrots in Ginger Coconut Sauce

Serves 4–6

2 tablespoons ghee
2 leeks, washed and cut into ¼-inch-thick half-moons
    (about 1½ cups)
3 large carrots, peeled and cut into ½-inch dice
    (about 3 cups)
3 cloves garlic, minced (about 1 tablespoon)
1 tablespoon grated ginger
2 tablespoons curry powder
1 14-ounce can coconut milk
½ cup vegetable stock
3 medium Yukon Gold potatoes, cut into ½-inch dice
    (about 3 cups)
1 cup frozen peas, thawed
½ cup roasted cashews, chopped
½ cup chopped cilantro
Lemon wedges
1 cup plain yogurt (optional)
Salt and pepper to taste

Heat ghee in large pot over medium heat. Add leeks and
cook 5–7 minutes or until soft. Stir in carrots, garlic,
ginger, and curry powder; and cook 2–3 minutes. Pour in
coconut milk and vegetable stock and bring mixture to a
simmer, stirring occasionally. Cover pot, reduce heat to
medium-low, and cook 15 minutes. Add potatoes, cover,
and cook 20–25 minutes more or until potatoes are
tender, stirring every few minutes. Stir in peas and cook
2 minutes or until warmed through. Season to taste with
salt and pepper. Serve warm over cooked soba noodles
or warm brown rice, with lemon wedges and a sprinkle
of toasted cashews and cilantro. Pass around a bowl of
yogurt for guests to add if they wish.

Part II

Communion

Perfect apple, pear, and banana,
Gooseberry . . . All of these speak
Death and life into the mouth . . .

— Rainer Maria Rilke, *Sonnets to Orpheus*, I, 13

Chapter 6

FARM

We pull the fan-shaped leaves aside. Hiding underneath, we find our prize—lovely, round, light-green globe cucumbers. Matthew, Jack, and I take them one by one off the vines and put them in our baskets.

We are at Full Belly Farm, a 250-acre organic farm located in California's Capay Valley, an hour northwest of Sacramento. It's a hot July day—nearly 100 degrees. Even with our sun hats, water, and sunblock-soaked skin, we won't last long. Farming, like many things, is more romantic from afar.

My idea of what constitutes real food changed 15 years ago when I started getting a weekly vegetable box from this farm. I remember opening my first box. The kale was so fresh, still so full of life, that it practically leapt into my arms.

Like a homing pigeon, I keep returning here. This place grows food that has nurtured my children since they were born. Now I want to show them where their food comes from and let them meet the people who grow it. But I'm also after something else. I've been searching for a balanced way of eating; I've been asking myself, how can I eat less of the foods that loosen my inhibitions? Now I want to learn about the foods, the processes, and the rituals that bring me closer to my food sources and back into balance—like eating vegetables and getting my hands in the dirt. And so, I'm starting here, at the farm I have come to love.

When we pulled in, Judith Redmond, one of the owners, greeted us. She still had some things to do, so she told us to explore on our own and meet her later. We meandered off and discovered this field of cucumbers.

After a mere 15 minutes, the heat bests me. As the boys continue to work, I walk over to a nearby oak tree and rest in its shade. Nellie, Chips, and Salsa, three of the farm's raucous band of dogs, join me. One of them catches the scent of a gopher and starts digging furiously near the trunk of the tree. The others follow and dirt flies. A farm worker at the other end of the field sees I'm knocked out, walks over, and hands me a piece of homemade bread. "Gracias," I say.

I nibble on the bread, then lie down on the ground and stare at the wide blue sky. A four-winged dragonfly flies over my head. Then another. I look around and there are dragonflies everywhere—hundreds of them. I feel like I've stepped into a film by the great Japanese animator Hayao Miyazaki, except the magical, iridescent flying machines careening madly about are real.

How different the world was just an hour ago.

The only hotel in the area is a giant casino, so that's where we spent the night. The lobby is filled with more than 1,000 slot machines as well as tables for craps, roulette, poker, and baccarat. Lights flash, smoke fills the air, and the machines incessantly bling. As we make our way through the lobby to leave for the farm, Jack looks at the hundreds of people already playing slots and says, "They don't look happy. But they look determined."

They are. Gambling doesn't interest me. But I do understand obsessive behavior. Over the course of my life, I've shopped more than I needed and overeaten on more occasions than I can possibly count. I understand the desire for distraction and the urge to zone out. I know too well what "I can't stop" feels like.

But not at this moment, not with these dragonflies. One has more purple on its wing, another more green. I'm grateful to this farm—it preserves the space for magic to emerge.

The sun has finally made the boys tired, too. They stop their work. We gulp some cool water and move on. Because it's summer, the farm's activity is at its peak. Everywhere we see fields overflowing with produce— corn, tomatoes, green beans, eggplant, peppers, peaches, and many different varieties of squash, including the small crooknecks that look like baby swans.

We walk into an apple orchard, and I'm happy for its shade. There's a chicken coop nearby, and we are met with clucks. "Let's get some eggs," I say. We enter the coop, and I reach under the warm body of a fat hen. She instantly pecks me. Ouch! I try again and get henpecked once more. I give up.

As we wind our way past the Asian-pear orchards and cornfields, I wonder about the meaning of progress. By the time I was a young girl, frozen and canned food was the norm. Part of its purpose was to free women from the kitchen so they could work—a good thing. In our culture, money is power; and women need to earn their own. But as packaged food and fast food became the norm, more people, regardless of their sex, forgot how to cook. Along with good nutrition, vital knowledge was getting lost. Many people began to believe that you needed to turn to science, which broke down food into quantifiable nutritional components, to understand how to eat. People came to think you could isolate compounds, swallow them in pill form, and forget about eating whole foods. I don't buy it.

We reach the packing sheds. Tractors and other farm equipment sit in a lot in front. Inside there are bins of ice containing hundreds of ears of corn. There are a dozen varieties of melons, including galia, ambrosia, cantaloupe, honeyloupe, charentais, and canary. A woman washes eggplants in a big tub, their fat purple bellies bobbing in the water. A man cuts sunflowers and wraps them in bunches to sell at various farmers' markets.

Behind the shed we see a dozen tables topped with racks of sliced peaches and plums, drying in the hot sun. I try a dried peach. It tastes like concentrated sunlight. We take a few more to munch on as we move along.

Lunch is still an hour off, and the boys are ready for something different. Judith invites them to play on the trampoline behind her house, which is on the property; so we make our way there. While we walk, we spy a gigantic pig lying in a field.

"Would you look at that," I say.

"He's a whopper," Matthew replies.

I leave the boys at the trampoline and head up the main road. I'm glad for the solitude, for the time to meander and roam. Sprinklers suddenly turn on. A flock of startled birds emerges from the grass and takes flight. My skin is hot. It stings as I get pelted by the cold water.

I arrive at a peach orchard whose trees are filled with fruit as far as the eye can see. Some of the branches are so heavy that they have to be propped up by wooden supports. The red-yellow fruit with its oblong, crinkly green leaves looks beautiful against the azure sky. I reach up, take one, and bite into it—it's sweet, with creamy, white flesh.

This is what I hungered for but rarely experienced as a child. Though I never spent much time on farms, I do remember going to Van Riper's Farm in Montvale, New Jersey. Every Halloween, Van Riper's set up an elaborate stand with witches on broomsticks and goblins whose faces were drawn with a gentle menace. Van Riper's sold freshly made sugar donuts, tangy apple cider, and hard candy apples. I used to bob for apples in a large tin bin. But what I loved most were the pumpkins—giant orange orbs growing on stems from the ground. It was harvest time, and I wanted to wrap myself up in all things autumn.

I feel a gentle wind on my face as it sweeps through the valley. I get up and head back toward the kitchen for lunch, passing by a copse of pomegranate bushes whose fruit will be ripe in a few months. Nearby is a stand of plum trees filled with iridescent purple fruit.

Jack and Matthew are already seated at one of two long tables. We are joined by the farm's interns, along with Judith and her partners in the farm, Paul Muller, Andrew Brait, and Dru Rivers.

Lunch is colorful and abundant. We dig into red cabbage salad made with cucumber and peppers; roasted eggplant with onions; sautéed tofu and green beans in sesame oil; grilled bread with butter; ears of fresh corn; and my favorite, yellow and red tomato salad with basil and onions, topped with an olive oil and black-pepper vinaigrette.

The corn is especially juicy and sweet. Andrew asks Judith if she likes the sweetness level. She says she likes "cornier" corn. This begins a spirited discussion about the best-tasting corn, which leads to the subject of seeds. Full Belly often plants with heirloom seeds, old varieties of plants that are passed down from generation to generation. Heirlooms adapt well to their specific ecosystems, and they tend to be hardy and yield flavorful fruits and vegetables. And because there are so many varieties of these seeds, they protect the genetic diversity of seed stocks.

We talk about the rise of genetically modified seeds, which are patented and therefore owned and legally protected by the huge corporations that produce them. In many cases, farmers sign contracts in which they agree not to save and replant seeds, though farmers have replanted seeds since the dawn of agriculture. Sometimes these contracts also have other clauses, granting access to the farmer's land and business records.

"I'm surprised that anyone signs these contracts," Judith says.

I'm not. I know companies sell these seeds because they make billions of dollars doing it, and farmers use them because they boost yields and short-term efficiency. I'm sure some people at these companies believe they are doing the right thing, but patenting the very foundation of our food supply seems deeply short-sighted and wrong.

"There's no end to rationalization," says Paul. "Just convince yourself that you are feeding a hungry world.

Or tell yourself you just work there. Disconnection allows you to do many things. It lets you say, 'I'm not responsible for that.'"

The conversation saddens me, but this farm gives me hope. As I eat the last of my tomato salad, the fruit is so ripe that its juice spills down my chin.

• • •

It's a mid-July day, 1968. The air is hot and humid and the trees green and full. My sister, my brother, and I walk down the street, just past the New Jersey state line. We are off to buy tomatoes at the farm stand at the end of the road.

The giant New Jersey tomatoes are lined up on a weathered wooden table, watched over by an old woman with worn hands. We pay for our tomatoes and bring them home. We cut thick slices, which we dip in a plate of kosher salt. We eat them over the sink, their juice dripping down our faces and forearms.

These tomatoes are delicious and so different from the hard, anemic, three-in-a-plastic-pen ones from our local supermarket that I usually eat. When I first learned that tomatoes were a fruit, I refused to believe it—until I ate one from the stand at the end of my road.

I don't know then that this stand represents a last gasp for the area's local farms.

• • •

We all pitch in to clean up the lunch table. We scrape our plates into a bin that will later be added to the compost pile. Crackers, a large red tomcat, pulls one of the corncobs from the bin and starts licking it madly. I laugh—my old cat, Rose, who died years ago, used to love corn, too.

After lunch, we head toward Judith's house. It's made from straw bale, whose high insulation value keeps the house warm in the winter and cool in the summer. The moment I step over the threshold, I cool down. Judith asks me if I'd like some iced mint tea, which I gratefully accept.

She tells me that Full Belly now has about 1,400 members in its Community Supported Agriculture (CSA) program, a model of agriculture where you pay the farmer money in advance and get a weekly box of fresh produce in return. Fourteen hundred people is large for a CSA. Full Belly has about 50 core employees, rising to 65 in the summer. The farm is bordered by Cache Creek, which gets its water from Clear Lake and the Indian Valley Reservoir.

"We get our water from the creek and wells," Judith says, but she is worried. "Aquifers all over the state are in decline. We have to continually dig deeper. The water we are now using is over 2,000 years old. We know this because it's been tested for specific isotopes. Water is a serious issue, probably the issue of our lifetime."

I ask her why she remains committed to farming after so many years.

"Because what I do is at the nexus of so many huge issues," she says. "Agriculture plays a central role in climate change. It plays a central role in water quality. And it is the key factor in human health. This goes even beyond the issue of pesticides. Ask yourself, why does industrial agriculture only want to feed people starch and sugar?"

I nod, because I know what she's going to say next.

"Because it's subsidized and cheap," she says.

"With conventional agriculture, the power to grow, distribute, and market food is in the hands of corporations; and farmers are irrelevant," she continues. "But with the emergence of new farms and the growth of CSAs and farmers' markets, the farmer is once again front and center. We grow, market, and distribute all the food ourselves. It's an integrated system, and it makes the economics work for the customers and the farmer."

Her words remind me of something the poet farmer Wendell Berry once said: "Eating is an agricultural act. . . . Most eaters, however, are no longer aware that this is true. They think of food as an agricultural product, perhaps, but they do not think of themselves as participants in agriculture."

That's why I'm a member of this farm. By supporting them, I not only participate in agriculture, I also support a system that's good for the farmers, good for my family, and therefore, good for me.

The afternoon sun shines through the window. I know Judith has many more things to do before her day is over, so I thank her for her time and generosity and gather my things to leave.

On our way to the car, the boys and I bump into Paul. I take the opportunity to ask him the same question I asked Judith. What keeps him so committed to this work?

"It's simple," he says. "I keep at this because of a basic truth. We live in a deep ecology system. If you have healthy soil and microorganisms, you have healthy food. This is an agriculture based on mutual respect.

"Everything is interdependent," he continues. "Every system—the sun, the soil, the plants, and the rain—everything. When one piece is not considered, the other parts suffer. The bottom line is: if you're buying food, you're responsible for the long-term maintenance of this system."

There is an order to life here that makes sense. You see it everywhere—in the land that is healthy because it is well taken care of and in the beauty of the crops. Everything is composted. Nothing is wasted.

Perhaps I vaguely sensed all this 15 years ago when I joined Full Belly and started eating its produce. But I can't say any of it was explicitly clear to me. Here at the farm, the connections I'm looking for are all around.

"When we try to pick out anything by itself," John Muir famously said, "we find it hitched to everything else in the universe." I'm beginning to understand how what he meant applies to what I eat. I've been picking food out by itself for too long. What I want to explore now is how my food is hitched to everything else.

• • •

Tomato, Basil, and Onion Salad with Fresh Mozzarella

Serves 4

½ small red onion, peeled and thinly sliced (about ½ cup)
4 large ripe tomatoes (about 2 pounds), cut into bite-sized
    pieces; Brandywines are especially good
4 ounces fresh mozzarella, cut into bite-sized pieces
1 cup cleaned basil leaves, cut into chiffonades
3–4 tablespoons good aged balsamic vinegar for drizzling

Vinaigrette:
3 tablespoons good-quality extra virgin olive oil
1½ tablespoons lemon juice
1 garlic clove, minced (about 1 teaspoon)
Salt and fresh cracked black pepper to taste

Place vegetables, mozzarella, and basil in a bowl. Whisk
together all ingredients in vinaigrette. Pour over salad
and add salt and fresh cracked black pepper to taste.
Drizzle aged balsamic vinegar over salad before serving.

Chapter 7

FORAGE

The Berkeley Hills are dry. I'm collecting wild edible plants with local forager Iso Rabins in Tilden Park, just east of San Francisco. It's early summer and the pickings are slim. We're between seasons—the mushrooms and miner's lettuce are gone, and the berries have yet to arrive.

"We can eat that," Iso says, pointing out a patch of wild artichokes. They are wicked-looking, like the cultivated artichoke's evil twin. They stand atop five-foot-high stalks, each bract punctuated with a lethal spike. I approach with caution.

Iso reaches out and, holding the stalk carefully, cuts the artichoke off with his shears, then drops it into his sack. Though the artichokes are plentiful, we hew to one of the main laws of foraging: take only a small amount and leave the rest.

I ask Iso why he became a forager, and he tells me that he likes to be self-reliant. "For millions of years, we were hunters and gatherers," he says, as I put the last choke into my bag. "But now, food for most people comes from a supermarket. Without the necessity of gathering food, people no longer think that the edibles they find in nature are food." This is why I'm here, I tell him, to remind myself that food doesn't come wrapped in plastic and that nature is generous and food is all around us.

He nods. "Foraging for wild food connects us back with the land," he says as we climb down the scrubby hill and make our way back to the path, "with something primal. Something we shouldn't lose."

I have a glimpse of what he might mean. Tilden Park is important to me. Its 740 acres lie just up the hill from where I live. I've been coming to this park for more than 15 years. I've watched my boys take some of their first steps here, toddling off to see the snowy egrets and blue herons diving for fish on Jewel Lake. I remember hiking here with them once in early spring and finding some delicious wild sorrel and tiny oval-shaped chickweed, as well as miner's lettuce, with its beautiful heart-shaped leaves. In the late summer, we often gather buckets of blackberries. Tilden is more than beautiful: it offers some sense of the wild.

"Wild edibles love areas with dappled sun." Just as Iso says this, he points out a wild radish—a tall plant with dark green serrated leaves. He plucks off a leaf and gives it to me to taste. He nips some tiny yellow flowers off the top. "If you think the leaf was strong, try this," he says. I pop the flowers in my mouth and gasp.

The sharpness of the flowers is intense, on the far end of the spice range. Wild foods are not like processed foods—they have not been concocted to please the mass market.

We pull some of the leaves off the plant and move on to other wild radishes we see farther down the path.

"That looks edible," I say, pointing to a weedy plant growing close to the ground.

"That's yellow dock," he says. "I think."

"Think?" I ask.

"Yeah, think," he says with a smile. "It might be edible, but then again . . ." He grabs a few leaves and puts them in his bag. "I need to bring them home and identify them first."

I'm relieved. Another rule of foraging is to be sure; and if you're not, don't eat it. Which is why I find it interesting when Iso tells me that he not only forages for mushrooms, which are notoriously difficult to identify, he also sells them to various local restaurants.

"Any deaths?" I ask.

"Nope," he says. "But I only forage for six varieties. Once you've identified a plant, it's yours forever."

I spy a blackberry thicket still topped with white flowers. "It's too early for them," I say, disappointed.

"Look again," he says.

I do; and I see a few tiny, purple blackberries peeking out here and there. I carefully pluck some—blackberry vines are thorny, and I've spilled blood on more than one occasion trying to get at them.

Berries are always best eaten right off the vine. And there are so few, there's no sense in saving them for later. I put one in my mouth. It bursts with the taste of flowers and the promise of summer. We scan the path and parched hills for other plants but see little more to add to our bags.

"We're between seasons," Iso says.

I planned to make a meal out of our foraged food, and this just isn't enough. "What should we do now?" I ask.

"What about urban foraging?" he says. "There's a whole lot of food out there."

I'm game, so we turn around and head back to my car.

As we walk, kicking up dust with each step, I think about the wild radish leaf—how it lit a small fire in my mouth. Its potency stirs a kind of longing. Maybe that's what Iso meant when he said foraging connects us with something primal, something we shouldn't lose.

He is not the first to express this thought. In his seminal work *Stalking the Wild Asparagus,* Euell Gibbons wrote: "We live in a vastly complex society which has been able to provide us with a multitude of material things, and this is good, but people are beginning to suspect that we have paid a high spiritual price for our plenty . . . don't we sometimes feel that we are living a secondhand sort of existence, and that we are in danger of losing all contact with the origins of life and the nature which nourishes it?"

Maybe that's the beauty of wild foods: they bring us back to basics.

• • •

"Clean your house," my acupuncturist instructs me. It's 1995, and I'm 35.

"This is my first mushroom trip, and this is the only advice you can offer?" I ask.

"It's good advice," he says. "Dust balls can be distracting.

"Also," he adds, "drink a lot of water. And if you feel yourself moving in a bad direction, eat something. You'll come down faster."

I'm grateful for his guidance, but I was hoping for something, well, a little less prosaic.

He thinks for a minute, then adds, "Set an intention for your trip. Ask a question that's meaningful. Seek out something you've been longing to find."

I mull this over as I dust, sweep, and mop. I place bouquets of fresh flowers throughout our San Francisco flat. I put a pitcher of water, glasses, apples, and a loaf of oatmeal bread on the table.

Next I remove the packet of mushrooms from the refrigerator. Each is about two inches long, with a bone-colored stem and a shriveled, coffee-colored cap. They seem old, ancient even. In a way, they are. Humans have long searched out altered states, and hallucinogenic mushrooms have often been our capable guides.

I take out a couple of stems, place them in a ceramic teapot, add boiling water, and let them steep for a few minutes. I decide to drink only a small amount. I want to be careful since this is my first (and, it turns out, my last) trip.

I decant the tea into a mug and take it out back to our deck. Though Scott understands my desire to try mushrooms, he doesn't share it, so I'm doing them alone. It's a beautiful, clear morning. I take a sip. Such a bitter brew! A few dollops of honey would probably have helped. I have figured out my intention, deciding to go for the big question.

"What is the meaning of life?"

I'm serious. I figure if you're going to trip, then really go for it. Maybe nothing will come to me, but you never know.

As I finish the last of my tea, my cat, Rose, comes out and rubs her head on my leg. I scratch behind her ears, her favorite spot. A breeze kicks up, and I feel the wind touch my face. Fifteen minutes have now passed and our yard is humming with life. The bees buzz merrily, flying from flower to flower in some intricate dance

I can't decipher. Birds sing, chirp, and tweet. The leaves themselves start to shimmer and dance.

Maybe eating a psychedelic mushroom is my version of taking the host. Like the wafer and wine becoming the body and blood of Christ, the mushroom has become a way to step directly into the divine, which for me is the miracle of nature.

Our friend John made us a mix tape when we got married. He labeled it "Honeymoon Love Songs," and we listened to it as we drove across New Mexico. I remember falling under the spell of its sonorous, stirring tracks, which included compositions by Henryk Gorecki and John Lennon. I remember being deeply moved by it and want to hear it again. I go back inside and pop the tape into a cassette deck.

Since I've taken a small dose, the auditory and visual effects of the mushrooms are gentle but still potent. I lie on our bed, staring at the Navajo rug hanging on the wall. The light blue, dark brown, and white natural dyes form a ziggurat pattern against the coffee-colored background. The patterns begin to dance, the border of one color spilling over into the next. The whole rug seems to be breathing. All my senses are heightened. Colors shimmer, objects dance, sounds are amplified. I hear the whoosh of my blood as my heart pumps it through my body.

Several hours have now passed, and I feel happy. I haven't figured out the meaning of life, but maybe there is no single answer. Maybe recognizing the moments when I'm happy is enough. Then, from my cassette, I hear John Lennon singing "Love."

The song plays. Minor chords move to major chords and back again. I begin to cry. Music often softens my heart.

His words speak to me. Love *is* real. And nothing is more important. I cry some more.

My heart feels fully open. I have found what I came for. The meaning of life is love.

I also catch a glimpse of something else that will take me many more years to really learn: that food is not love. Food is food.

• • •

"Let's go visit my friend's loquat tree," Iso says. He tells me his friend's tree is huge, with lots of fruit. I agree, glad that perfectly good fruit won't go to waste.

We drive down from Tilden Park into town and park in front of a light-blue Victorian with white trim. His friend isn't home, so we walk through a gate and head into the backyard, which is scattered with balls, tricycles, and picture books.

"Holy shit," Iso says softly. A giant loquat tree stands in front of us, at least 30 feet high. Clusters of small, downy, yellow fruit grow at the end of each branch amid big, waxy, dark-green leaves. There must be thousands of fruits on this tree. I walk closer, about to pluck one off to taste, when I hear a soft *coo*.

To the right and the left of the tree are coops—one with roosters, the other with chickens. The roosters peck their heads toward me; their red combs stand proud while their wattles flap. The chickens, who come in shades of white, brown, and black, cluck and coo. Maybe they're hungry? I grab some loquats and shove them through the chicken wire. They peck happily at the fruit.

I bite into one. It tastes something like an apricot but not as floral. I gaze up at the tree and my mouth begins to water. Fruit lust is setting in. I must be careful. I've given in to fruit lust before. One time I picked 45 lemons off my friends' lemon bushes and drank lemon water for the next three weeks.

I start plucking fruit from the lower branches. Iso, who is 20 years my junior, grabs a ladder, climbs it, and then scrambles onto a branch. We start filling our bags, one after another. There are so many loquats on the tree that our five full bags don't even make a dent.

• • •

The garden behind the old couple's home is brimming with food: apples, blackberries, cucumbers, green beans, peppers, and tomatoes. It is summer in the Blue Ridge Mountains of Virginia. I'm 15 years old, spending the summer in Charlottesville, volunteering for a teen program that fixes houses for the poor.

I want to experience something completely new and different from my life in Rockland County. I barely know how to use a hammer or a saw, but I know I can figure it out. And Virginia is far enough away to feel like another world.

I swim naked with friends in a quarry, trying to ignore the slimy bottom and the occasional eel slithering past. I lose my virginity with a slender boy with long brown curls. We sneak out of our dorm at midnight and have sex on a blanket in a garden filled with rose bushes. I'm not in love—I'm impatient. After it's over, I feel sad. I wish I had waited for love.

I work with a crew whose job it is to build a wheelchair ramp from the sidewalk to the front door of an old couple's home. The house is tiny, maybe three rooms, with no running water. Antique glass bottles in cobalt blue, emerald green, and amber brown line their windowsills. When the sun shines through the window, the bottles light up from within, giving this modest house a strange opulence.

We work for several hours until the ramp is completed. The old couple is grateful and invites us to stay for lunch. I'm hesitant because I know they don't have much, including food. But I see their garden, with cucumbers and tomatoes practically leaping off the vines, and I'm reassured.

I go to the backyard and wash my hands in their creek's frigid water. When I come back in, the table is set with plates and forks. I ask the old woman if I can help her and she says, "No, lunch is almost ready."

She goes to her cupboard and pulls out two cans of Franco-American macaroni and cheese. She opens them, dumps them into a bowl, and brings them to the table.

My companions are quiet. I'm baffled. All that food right out back—why isn't it on this table? Then I get it. Though her garden is overflowing with produce, the old woman is serving us what she considers her best food. Canned, for her, means special. It's from the supermarket and costs money. She's more proud of what she can buy than what she can grow. This food is her offering, and I accept.

I take a small spoonful and put it on my plate. "Please take more," she tells me, so I do. I cut the gelatinous, cold macaroni and cheese and take a bite. I smile at her, and she smiles back. I finish what's on my plate.

• • •

Though we now have our wild radish greens, artichokes, and load of loquats, I need a little more food before I go home to cook.

Iso suggests heading down to the Berkeley Marina to gather sea beans, also known as pickleweed—a salty succulent that grows in marshy environments. He runs a wild-food CSA business, one of the first of its kind in the country. Twice a month, he forages for wild foods and sells them to the dozen or so people who have signed up to receive a monthly box. For his CSA boxes, he includes only sea beans that he has foraged from the cleaner waters up north, but he wants to show me what they look and taste like. Yet all I can think of is how polluted the Bay is and how, if I ate the sea beans, I'd also be ingesting toxic solvents and heavy metals. Iso says I'm being a little delicate, but he understands.

"There's a great patch of wild fennel behind my friend's chocolate shop," I tell him. I know this because when I was there the other day, Clive let me taste one of his experimental fennel truffles.

"Let's do it," he says.

As we get in the car, I ask Iso what's the wildest thing he has ever found.

"Probably these artichokes," he says. "You would never assume anything so deadly-looking could be edible."

We arrive at The Xocolate Bar. Clive is in the back kitchen, experimenting with more truffles. I introduce him to Iso and ask if we can forage some of the fennel.

"Be my guest," he says. "There's plenty of it."

There is; it's all over the place. I grab my shears and

start cutting the leafy fronds. "What am I going to make with all this fennel?" I ask.

"How about fennel pesto?" Iso suggests.

That sounds good; I can already imagine how it will taste.

"There are nasturtiums," Iso says, pointing. Sure enough, the land at the bottom of the hill is dotted with the vermillion and yellow flowers. I love their peppery flavor. "Have you ever tried the leaves?" Iso asks. I haven't, so I pop one into my mouth. No surprise—it's peppery, too.

We fill our bags with fennel and nasturtium. We are done for the day.

After dropping Iso off at the train station, I drive home and lay my bounty on the counter. I put a pot of water on to boil for pasta, then decide to tackle the most difficult job first. I don a pair of gardening gloves, pick up an artichoke, and gingerly cut the stem off with a sharp knife. Then I cut the thorny tips off the crown. Despite all my precautions, I still get stabbed; and it hurts.

With the crown off, I see the flower's purple interior. I smash it down to open up the bracts. I do the same with the other four, then put the chokes into a pot of boiling water, covering it with a lid.

Next I make a loquat crisp. Loquats are a small fruit, and to clean and remove the mahogany-colored seeds is a chore. After 30 minutes, I finally have five cups of cleaned, seeded fruit, which I then mix with sugar. I put this into a buttered baking dish; top it with a mixture of flour, sugar, egg, and butter; and put the dish in the oven.

After the pasta goes into the boiling water, I prepare the fennel pesto. First I wash and remove the lacy fronds.

Next I throw them into a Cuisinart with roasted walnuts, good Parmesan cheese, olive oil, and some garlic cloves. I pulse it all, then taste—delicious! Last, I sauté the greens with mushrooms, fold in some crumbled feta cheese, and spoon the mixture on top of some grilled ciabatta bread. I make a green salad and scatter the nasturtiums on top.

I drain the pasta, put it in a large bowl, and top it off with the fennel pesto. I have a lot of food; and tonight, with Scott traveling for work, it's just the boys and me. Will they even eat any of this?

We come to the table. The boys are dubious about this wild-food meal, but I dig in. The grilled bread with wild greens tastes like a forest—earthy and dense. The peppery nasturtiums bring the salad to life. The fennel pesto is chewier than I like; but the anise flavor blends beautifully with the nuts, garlic, and cheese.

As I eat, I think about a nettle dish I had recently at Oliveto's, a wonderful local restaurant. The nettles were chopped, cooked, and mixed with a béchamel sauce; then served like a terrine, with roasted hazelnuts scattered over the top. It was tasty and not cheap. It occurs to me that though wild foods are now chic, served in good restaurants across the country, not many people think to go out and find these foods, even when they are easily available.

The boys don't eat much of the main meal, but they can't wait for the loquat crisp. The cooked loquats look like marmalade and smell like apricot, citrus, and rose. The boys eat mouthful after mouthful and, based on this dish alone, declare my foraging expedition a success.

I pick up a wild artichoke and pull out a bract. It is nutty and delicious. I remember something Iso said earlier when we were up in Tilden: "Knowing what grows in a particular place grounds you to that place. Otherwise you can live in a place for 20 years and still not know it."

I agree. I lived in Rockland County for 20 years; and because my heart was closed, I never really knew it. But life has changed. I've lived in California for nearly a quarter-century, and the land is now in me. I finish the last of the artichokes—layer upon layer of wildness, sweetness, and thorns.

• • •

Simmered Wild Greens
with Feta Cheese

Serves 4 as an appetizer

¼ cup extra virgin olive oil
1 small red onion, diced (about 1 cup)
1 pound wild greens (or domestic greens), such as chard,
    spinach, arugula, or dandelion, washed and trimmed
⅔ cup chicken stock
½ teaspoon brown sugar
⅛ teaspoon nutmeg
½ cup crumbled feta cheese

Heat olive oil in large nonstick skillet over medium-high
heat. Add onion and cook 7–9 minutes or until soft and
starting to caramelize. Add greens and cook 3–5 minutes
or until just wilted. Pour in stock, sugar, and nutmeg and
bring mixture to a simmer. Partially cover pan, reduce
heat to medium-low, and cook 20 minutes or until greens
are tender. Remove pan from heat and stir in feta. Serve
over grilled or toasted crusty bread (warm or at room
temperature) or toss with pasta or use as a pizza topping.

Chapter 8

<><><><><><><><><><><><><><><><>

FEAST

I've never made a Passover cake; yet here I am with Grandma Ellen's recipe in hand, grinding nuts and whipping egg whites. I've never prepared a Seder, the traditional Passover meal before, either; but that's what I'm doing, all the while hoping that my 1960s-era *Maxwell House Haggadah* will lead me to the Promised Land.

Despite my inexperience, I'm happy to make a Seder for my family, but I also have a private agenda. I've often wondered if being raised Jewish affected what I eat: my love of heavy, fatty foods; my enjoyment of all things salty. Could there really be such a thing as cellular memory, the idea that our habits and tastes are stored on a cellular level, passed down from one generation to the next? For generations, my family has eaten a diet heavy on potatoes and cabbage, red meat and chicken—all foods I love. If I want to move away from fatty, heavy foods, am I swimming upstream against the current of my history? And if so, what will it take to change course?

Tonight's a good time to begin figuring this out. Passover tells the story of the Jews' exodus from Egypt; and as part of the Seder, I'm serving classic Jewish foods: brisket, matzo ball soup, gefilte fish. I am curious about what insights making, serving, and eating this food might bring.

"Where's the music?" Scott asks as he peeks into the kitchen. "You can't cook without music."

I turn to my sister, Robyn, who is visiting from Connecticut. "What will it be," I ask her, "Jefferson Airplane or Buffalo Springfield?"

"Surprise me," she says to me.

"Surprise us," I say to Scott.

Moments later, I hear the unmistakable opening notes of "Aqualung" by Jethro Tull. I whip the egg whites into frothy peaks as Ian Anderson starts warbling, "Sitting on a park bench . . ."

The egg I'm roasting on the stove for the Seder plate suddenly explodes. Fragments of burnt shell and cooked innards lie scattered everywhere. Oy. I clean up and take another egg out of the refrigerator. The idea of boiling, then roasting, an egg appealed to me because the burnt shell would have looked attractive on the Seder plate. But forget it. This time I'll just boil it.

I'm nervous about my matzo balls. My mother, who usually loves my cooking, does not like my matzo balls. "They're too hard," she's told me on more than one occasion. "You could break a tooth on them." So today I'm taking no chances. I consult some old recipe books and add seltzer to the matzo mix, which, the books guarantee, will make them fluffy.

I get dressed. I put on my Grandma Ellen's diamond ring and the delicate gold and garnet ring Robyn brought back for me from England in the late '70s. I wear Scott's grandmother Freda's gold and pearl locket, in which I've put pictures of Matthew and Jack, and my mother's chunky gold chain bracelet. I also put on gifts from my children: an antique glass and brass necklace from Matthew and a pair of tiny, red, plastic heart earrings from Jack, presents from last Hanukkah. This is way more jewelry than I ever wear, and none of it matches, but never mind. I'm wearing it all as a way to symbolically honor my family and bring my ancestors to the table.

What are these holidays for, in the end, if not to reconnect us to our past?

• • •

I don't know much about my grandparents' lives but a few scattered facts.

My father's father, Joseph, was a dentist. He died when I was six. I believe he was born in Germany, though I can't verify this. Sometime before my father was born in 1926, Joseph changed his last name from Mitterstein to Macy. He married Elsie Bookstein that same year; and ten months later, my father was born. At some point, Elsie changed her name to Ellen. Her parents, Mania and Gertze, were Russian and emigrated to the States before she was born.

The day before our Seder, I take out a box of old photos to try to piece together their stories. In pictures, Ellen is always proper and perfectly coiffed. She wears pumps, stockings, gloves, pearls, and a hat. She has a formal, chilly presence. On rare occasions, she smiles. My mother tells me she saved her limited warmth for my brother, who she knew needed it more than Robyn or I did. She died when I was ten. Pictures of my maternal grandfather show a slim man of medium height. He was bald, had a mustache, and wore rimless glasses. I don't remember him well, but I have a lingering sense of his kindness.

There are many pictures of my father. There's one taken when he was a baby. His dimpled, chubby thighs peep out from his bloomers; his huge brown eyes are full of joy. In another, he's a somber boy of ten, wearing knickers and a cap. He stands between his parents in front of a big white house with a wraparound porch. In another, he's 14 and in military school. Thirty-five years later we visited West Point together, the first year the school started accepting women cadets. My going to military school made no sense in any way except that at 16, when I wasn't rebelling against my father, I was trying to win his respect; and West Point would have clinched the deal. After a brief visit, I saw what I already knew: West Point was out.

At the bottom of the box of photos, I find some pictures of me. I am eight months old and wear a tiny, white cotton dress, my head sprinkled with dark brown hair. I also wear a giant smile, and my eyes are full of joy. My father and I have similar eyes—big, brown, and happy. Maybe that's why his memory still haunts me. I look just like him.

I put the box of pictures away. I have to start getting the house ready for our Seder. But I realize this: I need to make peace with my father. And whatever emptiness his life and death left in me needs to be healed with something other than food.

• • •

Back in my kitchen, I'm attempting to take the Passover cake out of the bundt pan. God damn it, it's stuck. I'm irritated; but I smile anyway, remembering the stuck-to-the-mold flan I made with my mother. I take a butter knife and run it along the fluted edge, turn the pan over, and shake again. The cake doesn't budge. I'll have to serve it in the pan.

The doorbell rings. It's my in-laws, Coleman and Jean. Jean brings her homemade gefilte fish, which is to the jarred variety as wild salmon is to cat food.

"The horseradish is from the French Laundry," she says proudly, referring to the fine Napa Valley restaurant. One evening while dining there, Jean told the chef at the time, Corey Lee, that she couldn't find a fresh horseradish root. The next time she and Coleman ate there, Lee presented her with a pristine root, which she has now turned into horseradish for our Seder.

My mother arrives with her friend Vivian and my brother, David, who is as happy as I've ever seen him. He is content with his wonderful girlfriend, Zarin, who isn't here with him tonight because she's visiting her family in Iran. My mother brings the *charoset,* the chopped apple, nut, and wine mixture that is symbolic of the mortar that the Israelites used to make bricks when they were slaves in Egypt. She also brings her tasty cucumber salad, which, for this occasion, I've asked her to make with real sugar, not Splenda.

I'm in the kitchen, putting the finishing touches on my soup. The broth is golden and rich. At 48, I still want to please my mother. I fish out a ball and, with some trepidation, taste. It's light and fluffy—a matzo ball even a mother could love.

Scott's brisket, which he made earlier in the week, is delicious. He used his mom's recipe, which includes ketchup, Coke (regular, not diet), and ginger snaps. Though we are only ten people, he's made 12 pounds of brisket—Jewish portions, I tell him. He's also made a rice pilaf to soak up the gravy.

We sit down around the dining-room table, which is set with china and wineglasses and adorned with jasmine and geraniums from the garden. I welcome everyone and say how happy I am that we can be together to celebrate Passover. Scott pours the wine, and grape juice for the boys, and I lift my cup and say the Kiddush, the blessing over the fruit of the vine.

I take the parsley, or bitter herb, from the Seder plate and dip it into salt water, which represents tears. I break the matzo and give a piece to Scott, who then breaks it in half and wraps each half in a napkin to hide. These wrapped matzos are known as the *afikomen,* which the boys, in a traditional Passover game, will look for after the Seder is over. We bless the matzo.

The boys sing the four questions, which the youngest members of the table ask every Passover. "Why is this night different from all other nights? Why do we eat bitter herbs? Why do we dip them in salt water? Why do we eat reclining?" The rest of the Seder service answers these questions. They sing in Hebrew, their voices young and high. They are nervous and earnest. "I'm *kvelling,*" I whisper to my mother, using the Yiddish term for bursting with pride.

I promise a brief Seder, so I hit only the highlights. We read about how the Jews keep trying to flee but the

Egyptians keep bringing them back. Finally, God is fed up and unleashes a host of plagues; blood, frogs, boils, locust, hail, vermin, darkness—you name it, he brings it. As we recite each of these, we dip our pinkies in wine and splash a drop on our plates. We say more prayers and, in less than 20 minutes, brief by even the most impatient of standards, reach those blessed words on page 30 of the *Haggadah*—"The Festive Meal."

• • •

My mother is 13. It's the earliest picture I have of her. She is lined up with her two sisters and brother, in a field, all on their hands and knees, smiling at the camera.

My mother wears shorts and a short-sleeved shirt. She is all limbs and has an athletic, boyish figure. It's the summer, and her mother has promised to buy her a pair of roller skates if she drinks the cream off the top of the milk every day until school begins. My mother is so skinny, so uninterested in food, that my grandmother is worried and wants her to put on some weight. My mother accepts the deal, and though she hates it and it makes her gag, she drinks the cream every day.

At the end of the summer, she asks her mother for the roller skates—but my grandmother, for some reason, decides not to get them. "She broke her promise," my mother tells me. "I never forgave her, and I never forgot it." This will not be the last broken promise my mother will experience.

There's a picture of my parents, 12 years later, on their wedding day. They stand under a *chuppah,* a wedding canopy. My father's arm is in a sling because he's severed a tendon. My mother is in a suit and a hat. The wedding is small and understated. It is the second marriage for both of them—their first (childless) marriages having come to quick ends. He kisses her, and I sense that she is pulling back slightly, as if unwilling to give herself fully over to him. This would turn out to be a wise move. After they married, he had, I suspect, at least one affair and possibly more.

My grandfather Jacob Bogoffslovsky and my grandmother Celia Oberman emigrated from Poland around 1915. When they arrived at Ellis Island, they changed their name to Bogoff and settled in East Flatbush in Brooklyn. My mother was born there along with her older sisters, Betty and Loretta, and her younger brother, Stanley. Another brother, Emanuel, died when he was two. My grandparents were tailors; and along with sewing clothes, they also manufactured bags for Ronson lighters, and jewelry bags for my great-uncle Henry's rhinestone jewelry company, Jewels by Bogoff.

In her late teens, my mother modeled for catalogs and ads. I have one photo of her in a strapless black gown, her naturally light-brown hair dyed blonde and pulled back in a chignon. She wears a diamond bracelet and earrings, with a white fur stole draped over one forearm. Her nails and lips are crimson. She gazes at the camera with a bemused confidence. She looks beautiful. Her entire life, she has admired people who live "upscale" lives, perhaps like the one depicted in this picture.

There's my mother's high-school graduation picture. She has creamy skin and blue eyes and wears a simple wool dress, which she's adorned with a corsage. She is posed with her hands demurely clasped by her cheek. She is a well-behaved girl, but inside is something wild.

That year, she was named best dancer at Brooklyn's Tilden High. Her specialty was the Lindy Hop; and her dance partner was a boy named Nat, who was "too old to be around schoolgirls," she once told me, "but could he dance." Most Friday nights when she was in high school, my mother and her best friends, Rita and Lovey, would saunter down Pitkin Avenue in the Brownsville neighborhood to meet their friends. She's a tall, reedy beauty in the picture, and I can imagine her being trailed for blocks by hormone-packed Brooklyn lads.

All the Bogoff women were beauties. There's a picture of my aunt Loretta with her huge, gorgeous blue eyes. She married, and then divorced, Jack, a bass player whom she met in the Catskills. There's my Aunt Betty, 18 years old, in a swimsuit, sash, and tiara, newly crowned Miss Brooklyn 1939. She has dark red hair, blue eyes, and luscious curves. I adored her. She married my Uncle Phil, and they were married over 60 years until she died a few years ago while eating ice cream and watching Bill O'Reilly on Fox News.

"What foods did your mother make that you loved?" I ask my mother on the phone as I look through more pictures. I anticipate a romantic answer based on classic Ashkenazi food—borscht, a sorrel soup called schav, pumpernickel, rye bread, potatoes, dill, sausage, sour cream.

"My mother used to make me spinach and potatoes," she tells me. "That made me vomit."

Vomit?

"I didn't ask what you hated," I tell her, "I asked you what you loved."

She tells me she was just never hungry, never interested in food. I continue to press her until she finally says, with a sigh, "Challah. My mother made the most wonderful challah. Big, fluffy, braided challah."

But, she says again, "I just wasn't interested in food."

• • •

"Absolutely delicious," my mother says, devouring my matzo ball soup with abandon. My soup's a triumph.

Jack raises his glass of grape juice and offers me a toast for making a "wonderful Seder," his Grandma for her "wonderful *charoset*," his other Grandma for her "beautiful gefilte fish," and "Auntie Robyn for being here from Connecticut. And," he adds, "for cleaning up our house."

"*L'chaim*," we cheer, and clink our glasses.

Scott brings out his brisket and serves it. Robyn says it's the best brisket she's ever had. I agree. It's a little sweet, a little salty, and very tender. By the end of the evening, my sister, who eats modestly, has had three servings. My mother's eaten a lot, too. She may never have been interested in food before, but tonight, she is. "In my day, brisket was called 'deckle,'" she says, smacking her lips.

As I serve coffee, we talk about Seders from our youth. My sister, my brother, and I start reminiscing about the Seders we used to have with a family I'll call the Cohens. "They detested each other," I say, referring to Dr. and Mrs. Cohen. My sister and brother nod in agreement. I usually left those Seders swearing I'd never get married.

"What was your most memorable Seder?" Robyn asks.

Unquestionably, that was Israel, 1978.

• • •

I am on an exchange program between my local community college and a small college in Jerusalem. Although I'm still a senior in high school, I'm able to earn college credit by coming here to study Hebrew.

I leave for Israel in January, midway through the school year. Even though, in nine months, I'll be headed off to college in New Jersey, I have to leave Spring Valley now. I feel like a stranger in my family; and I hate everything about high school, even the building's ugly, squat appearance. My education has left me completely uninspired. I need distance to gain some breathing room and figure out who I am—and who I want to be.

The night before I'm to leave for Israel, I get into an explosive fight with my father. With a crushing feeling in my chest, I listen to my father belittle me and tell me he's not letting me go. My mother tells me to leave the room, that everything will be okay, and that I am still going to Israel; but I refuse to drop it—I can't take his abuse anymore. I snap. I raise my hand in the Nazi salute.

His face contorts with rage. He leaps up to throttle me. My mother throws herself between us. She has probably saved me from getting pummeled, though at 17, I'm old enough and strong enough to actually wallop him back. I'm conflicted. I hate him, but I'm mortified by my actions. I just want to get on the plane and leave.

The next day at the airport, I barely say good-bye to them. When I get to Jerusalem, I study Hebrew and go on class trips to the Negev and the Sinai. I go with friends into town for lamb kebab dinners. I go with another friend who is fluent in Arabic to the old marketplace known as the *souk,* where we buy a sheepskin coat.

He haggles and gets me a good price. When we are done, we drink sweet, thick mint tea with the shopkeeper. On some evenings, my friends and I go up to our dorm's roof and smoke hashish. I watch the sun set on the city, with its buildings made of golden stone, commonly known as Jerusalem stone; and now understand why this ancient land is called Jerusalem of Gold.

The school I'm attending runs a program that matches visiting students with families for Passover Seders. I'm placed with a family in Meah Shearim—the most religious section of the old city. I pass into the gates of this section, and I feel like I've stepped a hundred years back in time. Men in long black coats and fur-lined hats mill about. I'm dressed modestly, my arms and neck covered, my skirt long.

The Seder is conducted in Hebrew, which I mostly do not understand. Hours pass; it is nearly intolerable. I excuse myself to go to the bathroom; and in the bathroom, I turn the light on. I hear a shriek and what sounds like cursing in Hebrew. The mother of the family runs in, pushes me aside, and turns off the light. Good Lord, I forgot! I'm not supposed to turn the light on during the Sabbath. I apologize profusely, shut the door, and sit on the toilet in the dark.

I sit for as long as I can without being downright rude, then come back out. The Seder is still droning on. Finally, after five and a half hours, the Passover meal is served. I'm starving. The mother brings out the first course: a giant cow's tongue surrounded by a parsley garnish.

She slices up the tongue and serves me a slab. My stomach lurches. I simply cannot bear to even taste it. After pushing the food around my plate for a bit, and after the final prayers are said, I thank my hosts and flee. As I do, I imagine them rolling their eyes, wondering what kind of American heathen they've invited into their home.

A few months later, I return to the States. I'm grateful for my time in Israel because it convinces me that it's not my home. But neither is Spring Valley. If I'm going to find a place in the world, I'll have to create it myself.

• • •

Matthew finds the *afikomen* first. Scott has hidden it behind the toy robot that stands sentry on our stairs. Jack finds his next, behind the Buddha statue in our front hall. Coleman hands each of them a $20 bill.

The boys' jaws drop, as does mine. "Grandpa!" I say. "Such largesse!"

"And why not?" he asks, with a smile. My in-laws are always incredibly generous to our family and often indulge "the little bubbies," as they call the boys. Matthew and Jack rush over to him and pile on the hugs.

I serve the stuck-to-the-pan walnut Passover cake, which my sister remembers so fondly from childhood. She takes a bite and smiles. She knows I did this for her.

We end the evening with music. My mother has brought song sheets from a Seder she went to a few years earlier with Passover lyrics written to old show tunes. To the tune of "These Are a Few of My Favorite Things" we sing:

Matzo and karpas and chopped-up charoset
Shank bones and Kiddush and Yiddish neuroses
Tante who kvetches and Uncle who sings,
These are a few of our Passover things . . .

We all crack up. We finish with those classic end-of-the-Jewish-evening songs, Adon Olam and Ein Keloheinu. The Seder is over.

Our families begin to gather their things to leave. As we make our way to the door, everyone lingers. No one wants to be the first to go. We are holding on to something—our pasts, our traditions, this moment—just a little longer, because who knows how many more Seders we all will share?

I hug everyone and give an extra-long hug to my mother. She's getting older, and her body feels more fragile. I hand her a bag filled with food from tonight's meal—brisket; Passover cake; and of course, my matzo ball soup. I feel good feeding her, knowing she will enjoy this food for days to come.

As I listen to everyone talk, I realize something: that my lust for the heavy Jewish foods of my youth is less about the food itself than the memories those foods evoke. Tonight's brisket was delicious, but what I really enjoyed was hearing Scott's story of getting the recipe from his mother. The Passover cake is fine, but I loved hearing my sister reminisce about how special this cake was for her as a child. Food isn't the only thing that nourishes—stories nourish, too. Tonight was the first Seder I can remember where I didn't overeat. Perhaps the stories had something to do with it.

Jack and Matthew hug their grandparents one more time. I hope they'll remember this Seder. I'll make sure to keep telling them many stories. So that when they are older and I am gone, they'll remember how much I loved them.

• • •

Dayna's Matzo Ball Soup

Serves 6–8

1 4-pound organic chicken, rinsed and giblets removed
6 cups chicken stock
6 cups water
1 large onion
1 4-inch-square piece kombu (optional)
2 garlic cloves, peeled and smashed
1 bay leaf
1 teaspoon kosher salt
3 large carrots, peeled and sliced into ¼-inch-thick rounds
   (about 1½ cups)
2 celery stalks, diced (about 1 cup)
½ teaspoon turmeric
1 handful fresh dill, chopped
Kosher salt and cracked pepper to taste

Matzo balls:
2 eggs
2 tablespoons canola oil
2 tablespoons seltzer water or plain water
1 packet matzo ball mix (half a 5-ounce package)

Place chicken in large stockpot with chicken stock, water, onion, kombu (if using), garlic cloves, and bay leaf. Bring to a simmer over high heat, skimming any scum that floats to the surface. Add 1 teaspoon kosher salt. Reduce heat to medium-low and simmer 2 hours.

Meanwhile, make matzo balls. Whisk eggs well in small bowl. Whisk in oil and seltzer water and then stir in matzo ball mix. Place in refrigerator until ready to use.

Remove chicken from pot and set aside to cool.

Strain stock and return to pot with carrots, celery, and turmeric. Bring to a simmer over high heat. Reduce heat to medium-low, cover, and cook 30 minutes or until vegetables are tender.

Discard skin from chicken and remove meat from bones. Shred or chop meat, then add it back into pot. Add more salt and cracked pepper to taste. Raise heat to medium and bring soup back up to a gentle simmer. With wet hands, form matzo ball mix into smooth, compact balls ¾–1 inch in diameter (you should have about 10–12). Drop matzo balls into simmering broth. Cook until fluffed up, about another 20 minutes. Don't let soup come to a rolling boil or matzo balls will fall apart. If little bits fall off matzo balls, don't worry. The bulk of the dumpling will remain intact.

When done, serve in bowls and top with dill. If not serving during Passover, feel free to add ½ pound of your favorite cooked pasta. Makes about 11 cups.

Chapter 9

PATIENCE

Yeast intimidates me. It seems so temperamental, so unpredictable. When yeast works, it's magic; but if you add too much, the dough takes over your kitchen. Too little, and your bread's a flop. If the temperature of the dough is off, the yeast grows too fast or too slow. I don't make bread because it's finicky and because it takes so much time. It's the original slow food. Baking bread requires qualities that I generally lack—patience and a willingness to cede control. But I suspect it's precisely these qualities that I must cultivate to get my eating back into balance. So here I am, about to bake bread from scratch, with Bill Briscoe, owner of The Bread Workshop, a restaurant and bakery in Berkeley.

"Brioche is a challenge," Bill says. "We'll probably make a mistake, but how else do you learn?"

The bakery is a white, airy space filled with warm, yeasty smells and the hum of machinery. It lies adjacent to the restaurant, which serves organic, sustainably raised food. We gather our eggs, butter, flour, and other ingredients and line them up on a large butcher-block work surface.

Bill begins cracking the eggs into a stainless-steel bowl. He is a double-fisted cracker. I can tell this makes

him happy. He's a typical harried small-business owner
—since we've begun, his staff has interrupted him several times. But baking seems to please him. With each successive crack, he relaxes and smiles more.

We measure and weigh each ingredient on a scale—in commercial baking, all measuring is done by weight, which is more precise than volume. Maybe that's another reason I don't bake: I've never liked measuring ingredients. It offends my inner anarchist. Instead, I estimate, then throw.

Bill grabs a giant bin filled with organic flour and weighs out one and a half pounds. He then weighs the milk, the salt, the sugar, and the yeast. Finally, he weighs out over a pound of butter and cuts it into small squares. Brioche is rich bread—its high egg-and-butter content makes for a luscious and tender crumb.

Bill gathers all the ingredients on a large tray and brings them to an industrial-sized mixer on the other side of the bakery. I can already imagine the final product. He senses my impatience.

"Might as well relax, it's going to be a while," he says. "Making bread is all about making yeast happy, and you can't rush yeast."

"Besides," he adds, "baking bread is not just chemistry, it's also creative. Why not enjoy the process?"

• • •

I'm nine years old and home sick. I turn on the TV to watch a soused Graham Kerr, the "Galloping Gourmet," discuss the virtues of butter and cream. I am suddenly seized by a fit of inspiration to create my own gourmet dish, Salami en Croute. Never mind that I don't know a thing about dough.

I pour some flour into a bowl, add an egg, and mix them together. I take out a pan and throw in a hunk of margarine along with chunks of Hebrew National salami. As the salami fries, I knead the dough with my fingers, then try it. It tastes like paste. Undeterred, I roll the dough out on a floured wooden board and cut it into symmetrical triangles. I place a dollop of the fried salami in the middle of each triangle and roll it up like a croissant. I tie each with a string, slather them all with a final layer of melted margarine, place them on a tray, and put it in the oven.

After 20 minutes, the hors d'oeuvres have nicely browned. I take them out and try one. It's disgusting.

But I'm proud anyway. This is so much more fun than just popping a Swanson's frozen turkey TV dinner in the oven! And I relish creating a dish entirely from my imagination rather then just removing one from a box.

• • •

Bill places the flour into the large mixing bowl and adds the sugar, milk, eggs, salt, and yeast. As the paddle swirls back and forth, he explains how mixing forms gluten, creating the structure that captures the yeast's gases inside the bread. He tells me it's important to get the gluten level just right; and; if handled too much, the dough will be tough. He turns the mixer off and grabs a small piece of dough to test. It rips too easily. That means it doesn't yet have the proper elasticity.

I add more butter. The lush fat feels wonderful in my hands. Since we're making this bread as an experiment and not for sale, I plunge my hands into the dough, mixing the ingredients together with my fingers. The dough feels burbly; and as the butter blends in, it takes on a glossy sheen. I feel like I'm in kindergarten playing with a softer, living version of Play-Doh. Bill tells me to take my hands out because he needs to mix it more with the paddles. After a minute, he tests another piece; and this time it stretches. It's ready.

He removes the dough from the mixer and places it onto the wooden work surface. He shapes it into a nice mound; puts it in a stainless steel bowl; and covers it, first with wax paper and then with plastic wrap.

"Now," he says, "we wait." I glance at the bowl nervously. I expect it to start frothing over the edge, like that classic episode from *I Love Lucy* in which Lucille Ball's dough erupts from her oven like a monstrous blob.

Two hours later (after I zip home, do some work, and make a few phone calls), I return to the bakery. The dough has doubled in size. The yeast is working; or, in technical terms, "proofing." In the process that's commonly referred to in home-baking recipes as "letting dough rise," yeast multiplies and converts glucose and other carbohydrates into carbon-dioxide gas, which makes the bread rise and expand.

Bill takes the dough out of the metal bowl and slaps it down on the counter. That looks like fun. Channeling the spirit of Lucille Ball, I pick it up and do the same. Slap, slap, slap! The dough is heavier than it looks, and it makes a satisfying *thunk*.

Per Bill's instructions, I start pressing the dough to release the carbon-dioxide gas that has built up. It feels spongy and alive.

He tells me not to handle it too much. "You are too hot to handle it," he says.

"So true," I murmur, laughing.

"I was referring to your body temperature," he says, smiling. "It affects the texture of the dough."

Bill takes out various baking trays—a small, classic brioche tin with fluted edges, a larger version of the same, and several loaf pans. He shows me a dough-shaping technique where you encapsulate the dough with your fingers and roll it back into itself in a ball. I try it without much success. His dough balls are neat, mine are lumpy. The first roll goes into the brioche tin and my lumpier one into the second. In classic brioche form, he rolls two smaller balls and places one on top of each of the balls already in the pans, like little hats.

We move on to the loaves. Bill slaps the dough a little more and then folds some into a rectangle. He shows me how to fold the sides in on themselves, then roll them up tightly, all the while stretching, not pulling, the surface.

He puts the first roll into a greased loaf tin. I do the same with mine. We fill five more loaf pans and then set them aside to rest. The dough needs more time.

"How do you know when the density of the dough is just right?" I ask as I make myself a cup of tea before sitting down to wait.

"You have to have faith," Bill says with an enigmatic smile.

• • •

It is almost midnight on Christmas Eve. I'm 23, walking with Stefan toward the church in the center of this old Swiss town. It's snowing. We walk past a graveyard filled with the bones of people who lived their whole lives in this small place. The air is cold. The ground is covered in a blanket of white.

In the church, we take our seats in a pew. The light of a thousand candles flickers. The church is so perfect, I feel I'm at a theater performance—which is fitting for how I view religious ceremonies. They are, for me, a kind of show. I don't believe that Christ was the son of God, but I believe he might have been a great man. And I'm happy to honor great men.

I don't believe in God either, at least not the God I was raised with. Though I went to synagogue from the time I was small, it was mostly for the music, and later as a way to meet boys. After my Bat Mitzvah, I continued studying, went on to be confirmed, and then moved to Israel for part of my last year of high school. I studied philosophy in college and went on to graduate school for a master's degree in philosophy, concentrating on ethics. Through it all, a belief in God eluded me.

Then, just after my father died and a few months before I left New York for Switzerland, I had a dream. I was on the telephone with my father. He was in Heaven, or wherever it is you go after you die.

"I want you to know I'm OK," he said. "Tell your mother that."

This didn't feel like a regular dream. This felt more immediate and direct. As his image began to fade, I thought, *If this really is a message from my father, what is the most important question I could ask?*

"Is there a God?"

"Yes," he answered, "but not like you think. It's

more like energy, or a force . . ." Then he faded, and the dream ended.

My father's words in that dream still ring true. I don't understand quantum physics, but the idea that everything is energy makes sense. I believe that when I die, I will be absorbed back into some greater energy that I cannot name or know. If that is death, and if that is God, I'm good with it.

In the church, I watch the parishioners fill the pews. Some are young and some are old. A few seem ancient, their bulky wool coats covering curved and hunched bodies.

Stefan takes my hand. He is so tall and so thin. Everything about him is bony. I think he must take refuge in my curves.

The church is ornate. The altar displays elaborate gold candelabras. A giant crucifix is attached to the wall behind it. The bishop and his priest enter. The bishop wears resplendent vestments—a creamy white chasuble, a kind of cape, covers his cassock. He wears a red stole with gold embroidered crosses down the front. His gold mitre sits regally on his head. He is carrying a thurible— a lanternlike silver metal box on a chain. He is speaking in Latin as he walks down the aisle, swinging the box gently forward and back. I get a brief whiff of something herbal. I look at my boyfriend, who says quietly, "Frankincense." He smiles and adds, "And myrrh."

The mass is conducted in Latin. Of course, I don't understand a word. I feel drowsy. It's late, and the candlelight and the Latin have a soporific effect. At some point in the service, the congregants rise to receive Communion.

I watch as a line of parishioners forms to receive

the Eucharist. I know that for many of these people, the wafers and the wine, through the miracle of transubstantiation, are the literal body and blood of Christ. I don't believe it, but I respect the symbolism. I am fascinated that people believe they become one with God by ingesting this food.

Should I receive Communion? What would show the greatest respect? I am a Jew, and an agnostic one at that. I decide that if there is a God, that being would want me to be truthful, not merely polite. I stay seated. I watch the old people receive the wafer and drink the wine. Some of their eyes are filled with tears.

After the service, Stefan and I walk out of the church. People greet him warmly. Though he no longer lives here, he grew up in this small town, with its giant mountains and lush fields. We walk toward his parents' home, our gloved hands intertwined. His mother, elegant and gray-haired, has made us a snack before bed. I drink a cup of chamomile tea brewed from flowers she grew and dried the previous summer.

I like his parents. I don't know them well, but I'm grateful for their kindness. There is real beauty in this house. The old wood gleams. Well-loved books line many shelves. Outside the kitchen window lies the now-dormant garden where Stefan's mother grows vegetables and herbs each summer. I trudge to the guest room upstairs and sink into the bed, which has a foot-thick mattress. I burrow into the warm wool blankets as my head nestles into the dense down pillows.

I think about the parishioners taking the host and becoming one with God. If only it were that easy for me. Through food, I have tried on occasions too numerous to count to connect with something larger than myself. But it has never worked.

The last thing I hear before sinking into sleep is the tinkling of cowbells in the distance.

• • •

"Impatience is my demon and my savior," Bill says as we sit at a table in his restaurant, drinking tea and waiting for the bread to rise some more. "Inactivity is hard for me, so slowing down for bread is hard."

I look at my watch. We've been at this for seven hours. Jesus, it's taking forever! My impatience, like Bill's, has both served and hindered me. Impatience got me my first job at 12, working the cash register at a local grill so I could start earning my own money. It got me to move to Israel in my senior year of high school so I could leave home early rather than wait for graduation. It got me to finish college and graduate school in five years so I could get a job, become financially self-sufficient, and begin living my own life.

But impatience is also my demon, especially with food. When I'm hungry, I can scarcely wait to eat. If I have a craving, I usually satisfy it, quickly, instead of waiting it out.

As Bill and I drink our tea, we talk about how getting closer to your food can change your relationship with it. I tell him that's why I'm here, to get closer to yeast. He tells me a story.

"In the mid-'80s, I worked in a French restaurant in San Francisco. The chef wanted to make turtle soup, so he sent me to Chinatown to buy a turtle. I love turtle soup—it tastes of swamp and sea, so I was eager to learn to make it.

"To kill a turtle, you pour boiling water on it. It sticks its head out of the shell, and you chop the head off. Two of the cooks wanted to do it, but I could tell they thought it would be fun, and killing is not about fun. I told them to get lost, that I would do it myself.

"I poured the boiling water on the shell, the turtle stuck its head out, and I chopped its neck with a knife. But I was timid, and I only got it 75 percent through." He pauses. "I had to do it again."

I ask him how he felt about killing the turtle.

He doesn't say anything for a moment, then replies, "Melancholy. But," he adds, "it teaches you to respect your food."

We sip our tea, both of us a little forlorn. I keep thinking of the turtle with its partially severed head dangling from its neck. Bill just looks tired.

"Let's feel that dough," he says, eager to change the subject.

We take the dough out of the refrigerator. "Now it's too cold," he says. "We've now ensured that it's not going to be perfect."

He lets the dough warm up for another 15 minutes and then declares the loaves ready to bake.

We load the loaf pans and brioche tins on a large metal tray, giving each of them plenty of space. We give the bread an egg-and-cream wash; and finally, seven and a half hours after we began, the bread goes in the oven.

For such a basic food, I'm thinking, *this all seems pretty complex.* Then I remember a mountain campfire where I learned how simple bread can be.

• • •

Scott, the boys, and I are up at Lake Shasta in Northern California, camping with several families from the boys' school. Mount Shasta is magical. Next to its formidable strength and beauty, I feel small in the best possible way.

It's dusk. The last faint hues of lavender and white streak the sky. I walk over to the fire and see Greg, one of the fathers in the group, making flatbread. Fresh-baked bread? In the middle of the woods? The bread—just flour and water—is baking on a grill over hot rocks. "I learned this from the Bedouin when I lived in the Sinai in Israel," he says, as he slathers more olive oil on top.

When it's done, he takes the bread off the grill. The parents and kids gather around the fire and pass the platter around. I rip a piece off. It's wonderful. The bottom of the bread is slightly charred; and the center is chewy, with a lingering scent of smoke from the fire.

Someone pours a round of wine. Twilight creeps in. The first stars emerge. A parent asks me to play a song. I grab my guitar and, with my friend Ginny, start playing a plaintive rendition of Townes Van Zandt's "Pancho and Lefty." People join in.

The scents of Douglas fir, sugar pines, and western juniper fill the evening air. I've eaten many delicious meals created by good chefs in fine restaurants; but this bread, and everything about the evening—the trees, the sky, the music, the friendship—is more memorable and ultimately more satisfying. And I'm content.

• • •

Bill takes the brioche tins out of the oven. After they cool, he removes the bread. We sit down at the table; and with just a touch of fanfare, he cuts the brioche in half. Before we taste it, he says, "Like I said, it's not perfect. It's underproofed." That means the dough didn't rise long enough.

"It's not light enough," he adds. "There are too many strands in the dough. It has 80 percent of the spring it should have."

"Oh, well," I say gamely, "Let's eat."

I bite the little hat off the top of the bread. Maybe it is underproofed, and maybe it isn't springy enough. Maybe it's even a little too dense. But I love it. The crust is wonderful, and the flavors of butter and salt are balanced. Bill wraps up a loaf for me to take home.

When I walk in the door, the buttery, yeasty smell lures Scott out of his office. He has to get his hands on the bread.

He cuts a slice. "It's still warm," he moans. He takes a bite. He sighs.

I remember the cinnamon-raisin bread he baked for our wedding 16 years ago. "Cinnamon," he said, "so our marriage will be spicy. Raisins so it will be sweet. And whole wheat so our union will be hearty and healthy." I was moved then, and I'm happy now, to be married to this man who bakes bread for me.

"This brioche is crusty on the outside and warm on the inside," he says with his mouth full.

"Like someone I know," I reply, helping myself to a slice.

• • •

Simple Buttery Brioche Loaf

2 cups white flour
½ teaspoon fine sea salt
1 tablespoon white sugar (plus 1 teaspoon for
    proofing yeast)
1 packet dry yeast
2 eggs, at room temperature
2 tablespoons whole milk, at room temperature
1 stick unsalted butter (4 ounces), at room temperature

Egg wash:
1 egg
¼ cup whole milk

Mix flour with salt and 1 tablespoon sugar.

Proof the yeast: Bring 3 tablespoons of water to 115°F
and place in a bowl. Stir in 1 teaspoon sugar. Sprinkle
yeast gently over sugar water and stir until dissolved. Let
sit 5 or 10 minutes. The yeast mixture should be nice
and foamy.

Beat eggs, add milk, and mix in yeast mixture.

Form a dough: Put all but about ½ cup of flour mixture on a work surface and make a small well in the
center. Pour liquid into well a little at a time and stir
continuously in one direction with your finger or a fork
to gradually form a dough. This should take about 5
minutes. Knead this dough vigorously for another 10
minutes, adding flour from your reserve as needed to
keep the dough from sticking to the surface.

Incorporate butter: Keep kneading dough. Add butter, a
half-dozen almond-sized bits at a time, spreading it with

your fingers and then kneading it in. As you keep adding butter, dough should become satiny, almost shiny. As you go along, add in any remaining reserve flour. This should take another 10 minutes or so.

Form dough into a ball, lightly flour it, and put it in a bowl. Cover with a damp towel, place in a warm location, and let rise about 2 hours (more or less, depending on temperature), until dough has roughly doubled in size.

Lightly grease a small (5" x 9") loaf pan. Punch dough down, shape it into a log, and place it in loaf pan with seam down. Cover with wet towel once more and let rise 1–2 hours, depending on temperature, until dough fills the pan.

Add egg wash: Beat egg into milk and lightly brush on top of loaf.

Bake 25–30 minutes at 400°F. Brioche should be browned on top and bottom of loaf pan should sound hollow when you tap it.

Adapted from Bill Briscoe with special thanks to Scott.

Chapter 10

SLAUGHTER

I eat meat and so am something of a rarity here in Berkeley. I live among vegetarians, at a time when vegetarianism is on the rise. I understand and respect the case for it. But I've never wanted to give up meat. I enjoy it, and eating it now and then seems to work well for my body.

For a long time, this choice wasn't something I dwelled on. But recently, as I've begun to see my eating choices as part of a larger web of connections, I've found myself thinking differently about meat. If I'm not going to give it up, then I need to understand and take responsibility for the impact of my decision.

Mostly, our meat comes to us neatly sliced and wrapped in cellophane. But that's not how it starts out. Every bite of meat I take comes from a large animal that someone kills. Between the living animal and the plastic-wrapped cut of meat, there lies a mess of blood and bone and viscera. Mostly, we avert our eyes from that mess. I want to look, to bear witness, to feel the connection between my choice to eat meat and the animal that must die to provide me with it.

That's what brings me to Prather Ranch in Macdoel, California—east of Mount Shasta at the base of the

Siskiyou Mountains, near the Oregon border. I'm here to watch a steer slaughter.

The ranch spans 38,000 acres in two locations with two distinct climates: Mediterranean in the Sacramento Valley area to the south, high alpine in the north. The land is geographically isolated, a feature necessary for maintaining the ranch's closed-herd status. The ranch stopped bringing in new females for the primary herd in the 1970s and brought in the last bull in 1990. A closed herd allows complete tracking of an animal's health from birth to death, and it also decreases the risk of contamination from outside animals.

The ranch is owned by two families, the Rickerts and the Ralphs; the latter also owns the West Coast supermarket chain bearing its name. Prather produces certified organic beef that's also certified "humane raised and handled." This third-party certification ensures the humane treatment of farm animals from birth through slaughter, and it sets higher standards for slaughtering than is required by the federal Humane Slaughter Act.

If I'm going to watch a slaughter, I could not have picked a finer place. Each week, Prather slaughters about 20 "fat calves," or calves between 18 months and two years old. I'm well aware that what I will witness is a vastly different process from what I would see in a concentrated animal-feeding operation, or a commercial slaughterhouse, where upwards of 50,000 cattle can be slaughtered a week.

When I started corresponding with owners Jim and Mary Rickert, Mary asked me one question: "Why do you want to watch a slaughter?"

I tell her that, for me to be a responsible consumer, I need to watch how that meat "gets from animal to plate."

"Well then, by all means, come and visit," she said. "And don't forget to bring a camera."

• • •

The truth is, I'm afraid. Will I gag? Pass out?

I say this to Mary the night Scott, the boys, and I arrive; and she offers to take me on an advance tour to prepare myself. We are staying in a house on the ranch directly across from the feedlot and the abattoir, or slaughterhouse. Mary meets us on arrival, along with Mark Estes, the feedlot manager. Mary is kind, with a frank, forthright manner. Mark is a taciturn young man with sandy blond hair and a handlebar moustache. He wears a cowboy hat and spurs. I ask him why he wears spurs, and he looks at me as if I'm daft. "For my horse," he says. "I wear them to ride my horse."

We walk by the feedlot. Mark points out a calf with the number 2025 on a tag hanging from her ear. "Watch her," he says, "that one scratching her belly. She has this tongue fetish." We watch; and sure enough, in a few seconds, the calf starts licking her mouth and nose with her long, velvety tongue. The first digit on the ear tags refers to the field in which the animal was born and raised, and the last three digits record the birth order. The year the calf was born is also indicated on the tag; and like this calf, I notice that most say 07.

Mark points out 20 fatted calves in a separate pen, waiting to be slaughtered tomorrow. "I pick them out," he says. "I'm the guy that says, 'You're going to die tomorrow.' But I don't let them suffer."

I look at the calves. They are gentle and beautiful. Mark and the Rickerts raise several breeds: the red-and-white Herefords and Black Angus, as well as a variation of the latter, known as Red Angus. They also raise Black Baldies, a crossbreed of Angus and Hereford. The calves are skittish around me. "It's because you're on foot," Mark says. They're not around people much; they're usually left on their own in the fields. When they do see people, it's usually on horseback or in a four-wheeler.

I notice that Mary is standing back. "I can't look the animals in the eye on Monday night," she says. I'm surprised by her admission of conflict. "I have to detach," she says. "But I also know these cattle have lived a bucolic life and have had the absolute best experience a bovine can have."

It's dinnertime, so the advance tour of the abattoir will have to wait. Jim and Mary have invited us to join their staff for a meal.

Scott, the boys, and I drive back down the long gravel road we came in on, a mile or so toward the hills to another part of the ranch. We park next to one of the ranch's old, original houses and walk to the field behind. I see picnic tables and two big tire swings, which the boys instantly claim. The fields are full of aspens and ponderosa pine and scattered with purple lupines.

Jim greets us. He is a tall, thin man with gray hair and blue eyes and, like his wife, warm and welcoming. We're joined by Chris and Lynnae, who drive the swathing machines that cut hay; Mark's wife and their two young daughters; and Ellen, who cooks for the farm, along with her young children. The ranch has two other visitors tonight: a doctor and a research scientist who are studying the use of bovine hemoglobin in the treatment of canine cancer.

We eat grilled hamburgers made from the ranch's beef, with roasted potatoes, pasta salad with artichokes, and blackberry cobbler for dessert. But despite the food's appeal, I eat little. My mind is racing ahead to the upcoming tour.

Dusk settles. We finish our meal, and I go to meet Mary in front of the abattoir. The 20 cattle destined for slaughter are still in their pen. They seem content.

As we walk toward the abattoir, Mary shows me the chute where the cattle will enter, a few at a time. The ramp is angled, so each steer can see only the one in front of him. The surface of the ramp is covered with nonskid padding. Much of the abattoir's design is based on the principles set forth by the well-known professor of animal science Temple Grandin, who has said that "using animals for food is an ethical thing to do, but we've got to do it right. We've got to give those animals a decent life and we've got to give them a painless death. We owe the animal respect." The angled chutes keep the cattle from seeing any machinery; and the ramp's surface, which prevents sliding and scrambling, keeps them calm.

At the end of the ramp is the stun box. It holds one steer at a time and is completely enclosed, except for a metal faceplate in the front wall where the steer's head goes. Outside the box, and out of the animal's line of vision, is a metal walkway where the stunner stands. He takes a knock gun; loads it with a 22-caliber blank; and in one quick movement, stuns the steer right between his eyes. The force of the blow renders the steer instantly brain-dead. When the steer falls, he hits a levered door that drops him to the kill floor.

Mary opens the door to the kill floor and asks me to take a deep sniff. "What do you smell?" she asks.

"Nothing," I say.

"Exactly," she replies. The abattoir is completely clean.

She shows me the cradle that will hoist the steer off the kill floor by his rear legs. When the steer is suspended, a worker will sever the steer's aorta. Once all the blood drains out, the worker will cut off the steer's head. Two more workers will then remove the hide and gullet. The steer will be hung up and eviscerated. A USDA inspector will be on hand during the entire process. Finally, the carcass will be sprayed with an apple cider vinegar wash to inhibit the growth of *E. coli* and then moved into a cooler, where it will be dry-aged for a minimum of two weeks before it is processed into different cuts of meat to be shipped out to market.

The abattoir is smaller than I expected. Prather is a small operation, and there are at most eight people on the kill floor at any time. Mary shows me the back door in case I need to take a break.

I walk back out the way we came in to look everything over one more time. By the stun box, Mary points out something I missed earlier. It is a plaque with these words by Temple Grandin:

> *I believe that the place where an animal dies is a sacred one . . .*
>
> *The ritual could be something very simple, such as a moment of silence. . . . No words. Just one pure moment of silence. I can picture it perfectly.*

• • •

I wake up with the sun. From our bedroom window, I see a car and a pickup truck drive slowly down the long gravel road. It's early, 6:30 A.M.; and the vehicles' head-lights are on.

A man in boots, holding a coffee mug, walks down the road. The cattle are spooked. They move away from him.

I go into our kitchen to get some coffee myself and prepare for the day ahead. From the window, I watch another man wearing boots and an apron herd some of the animals marked for slaughter into the abattoir. The other cattle make their way closer and watch. After a few moments they lose interest and turn away. One jumps on another's back in play.

6:50. There's a lot of action. Two Prather trucks and a car drive up to the abattoir. A woman with a clipboard comes out. Jim gets out of the truck. I feel my adrenaline rise. I'm anxious; I want to get this day over with.

"Are you scared?" Jack asks as he comes into the kitchen.

"Yes," I say. "Completely."

I pour myself a small bowl of cereal and sit down at the table. Matthew joins me.

He tells me that cows are his favorite animals. "They're big and slobbery and well tempered, and their hide feels soft," he says. He and his brother went to farm camp this summer and spent a lot of time hanging around cattle. "I love their noses and their thick tongues. They're not too graceful, but I think they're majestic."

He pauses, and then adds, "They seem dumb but are really smart. They form groups. They have emotions. They're funny. They're patient, and they're peaceful. Their peacefulness makes them majestic."

His words depress me. Cattle are wonderful crea-tures, and I'm about to see a few of them be killed.

I get dressed. I pack up my notebook and a plastic bag in case I retch. Scott and the boys will go spelunking in some local caves while I do my work. I kiss them as I leave.

It's now 7:30. Mary meets me in front. "Are you ready?" she asks kindly. I nod.

We walk up to the abattoir's back door. I pause, take a breath, and enter. She hands me a hard hat and plastic booties to put over my shoes. We walk slowly down the hallway, turn right, and pause before an open door.

"Okay," Mary says. "You can take this as slowly as you want. One step at a time."

I move closer. Before I see anything, I smell it. A combination of blood and the apple cider vinegar wash. It's an odd smell—metallic and astringent. I start to gag. I step into the hallway and then back outside. I take a deep breath, collect myself, and head back in.

This time I force myself to look. From where I stand, I'm watching the end of the process first. I see the Rickerts' son James picking up the organs of a newly gutted steer. He rinses the trachea, heart, liver, and lungs; and then sorts them into plastic vats. I look up, following the process back from the end to the beginning. I see a giant carcass, hung by its rear legs on metal hooks, already eviscerated. A man is spraying it with apple cider vinegar. The sight combined with the smell once again makes me gag, and I step back into the hallway again. After a minute, I return.

I look to the left of the cleaned carcass and see two workers gutting a steer's body cavity. The steer is hung by its hocks, and guts spill forth—stomach, heart, lungs. The organs glisten, different hues of red and pink. I find them strangely beautiful.

Further down, two men remove the hide from another steer. They slice through the fascia with a sharp knife. I am fascinated by this webbing that connects the inner body to the hide. Behind them, Jim is removing the cheeks from a severed head. Next to him is a USDA inspector.

I see a burly man in boots and an apron hang a steer that's just been stunned. He attaches hooks to the hind legs and the cradle whirs and lifts the animal up. The steer is brain-dead but technically still alive. The man steps in front of him and with a sharp knife makes a quick, long cut in the neck, severing the aorta. Blood gushes out into a five-gallon bucket on the floor. I watch the blood rise in the bucket until it hits the top, like a red river threatening to overflow its banks.

The man then takes his knife and starts severing the head. I know there's a method to this, but I don't know enough about bovine anatomy to understand it. The process takes about a minute, and the steer's head is off. The worker hands the head to Jim, who rinses it and takes the meat out of the cheeks.

The floor is a whir of activity. The workers' movements seem almost choreographed. Each step takes about ten minutes, and nothing seems hurried. The men obviously have done this many times; and their movements are efficient and quick, but calm. They are quiet and professional.

I stand there, watching it all now, smelling it all, and asking myself, *How do I feel?* I don't know. I feel numb.

Mary, who's been standing quietly beside me this whole time, asks me if I brought my camera. I find her commitment to transparency remarkable. I tell her no, and she tells me to go get it. So I walk out, retrieve it from the house, and come back in. I take photos—the organs, the vats, the carcass, the evisceration, the hide, the head, the blood—all of it.

But I'm not done yet. I still haven't seen the stun.

• • •

I pull up a stool and sit, waiting for the stunner, a man named Scott Towne, to come back in from the kill floor. The chute where the cattle are waiting is mostly blocked from view, except at the bottom, where I can see their hooves.

Mary makes sure I settle in, then tells me she needs to leave. She can't watch the stun, she tells me. "I could be a vegetarian," she says, her eyes filling with tears, "but my body needs the protein." She turns and leaves.

Towne walks up to the top of the chute and prods a steer forward. He rinses him off with water, then pushes the others back. The room is quiet except for the whir from a generator. Towne moves the steer into the box and closes the gate, which is solid metal—the steer behind will see nothing.

The steer puts his head through the metal faceplate. I get up from my stool and stand in front of him.

Towne is standing above and to the left of the steer. He loads the knock gun. With one swift move, he brings it above the steer's head directly between the eyes and pulls the trigger.

There's a loud bang. The steer's eyes roll back into his head, and his body sags. His lips twitch and he starts to froth at the mouth, an involuntary reaction of the body shutting down. His eyes roll back down, no longer seeing anything. Towne waves a handkerchief in front of them to check for any reaction. If the steer's eyes follow the cloth, he's still conscious. There is no response. The steer is brain-dead.

The 1,200-pound animal sags farther, falling to the ground. His body hits the levered door and falls through to the kill floor below.

Watching the stun—the moment when a sentient being's life ends—is extremely difficult. I feel very sad. Consciousness, and life itself, is a precious gift. This steer did not choose this end for himself, nor could he have chosen it. I am not convinced we have the right to make these decisions for other species.

Towne goes onto the kill floor to hang the steer up and sever its aorta. In the Prather operation, each worker does more than one thing. In a commercial slaughterhouse, workers do only one job, which makes the process much less personal. To succeed in supplying huge quantities of cheap meat to consumers, the meat industry depends on depersonalization of vast proportions— not only for the workers who harvest the meat but also for the consumers who buy and eat it.

Towne comes back in for another stun. He moves a steer up, sprays it with water, and prods it into the box. I take my place in front of the steer. Towne loads the knocker. I look into the steer's eyes. They are gentle, looking directly back at me.

As we look at each other, I make a promise: to never be cavalier about eating meat again; to eat less of it; and when I do eat it, to honor it. And to support places like this, which take such fine care of their animals in life and in death.

I've been watching now for close to two hours. Though the slaughters will go on for another two, I'm spent. I walk through the kill floor for the last time. James is carrying some organs to be rinsed.

"Did you get what you need?" he asks.

I nod my head yes, and he adds, "We have a job to do, and we do it in the best way possible."

I nod again. I believe this is true.

I walk back to the hallway, take off my booties and hard hat, and walk out the back door. Big plastic bins of offal are piling up—stomachs and other parts of the cattle that will not be taken to market. It will be carted away later by a company that renders it into tallow to be used in other products.

Another two bins are filling up with hides. Hundreds of flies swirl around the bins, feeding on the remnants.

• • •

Mary and I walk back to the house and sit on the picnic tables out front. A man I saw working in the abattoir joins us. He wears a blue oxford shirt with his sleeves rolled up, and he smells of blood and apple cider vinegar.

We are all quiet. I hear a shot ring out. "It's the bull," Mary says. The knock gun is not powerful enough for a bull's thick skull, so instead, they have to shoot him with a real bullet. The ranch adds bull meat to its hamburger meat to enhance the flavor.

The bull is the last to be killed, and Mary says that the crew will be eating lunch soon. "Make sure you go and talk to them," she says. I look over at the pen. It is now empty. The slaughter is done for the week.

A large truck pulls up to the back of the abattoir. A

man gets out and starts dumping the giant bins of offal into the truck's rear cabin. After a few minutes, he's done. He closes up the back of the cab and drives away.

Mary and I make our way into the small lunchroom that abuts the abattoir. She introduces me to Towne and his crew—Luke, Anthony, and Butch. Towne runs a mobile slaughtering business, going to ranches in the area and either slaughtering the animals himself or assisting. They're a hungry group. Ellen, the ranch cook, has put together a taco salad with tomatoes, beans, chopped meat, tortillas, and lettuce. The men's plates are piled high with food. Mary asks me if I have any questions for the crew. I feel awkward. They're eating lunch. They're tired. And I'm not even sure what's appropriate to ask.

Towne seems to recognize my reticence and says simply, "I grew up on a ranch. All this is second nature."

He's kind. He is making it easier for me.

"What's most interesting for me," he continues, "is when that 1,200-pound animal goes down, the air comes out of his body, and he lets go of a big sigh."

He digs into his taco salad. "It's important to keep the animal calm," he says. "It's safer, and the meat tastes better."

I mention that I've seen video footage of sick cattle who can no longer stand up being led to slaughter, even though that's against the law. "The meat is redder and tougher," says Towne, "because the animal's cortisol levels are too high."

I ask if there's anything out here, in a place like this, that could agitate a cow.

"A full moon," Towne replies. "I've seen cattle get all riled up when the moon is full."

• • •

Later, Ellen serves the rest of the guests lunch. As I stand in the guesthouse kitchen waiting for the food to be put out, Jim hands me an ear tag as a memento. It's number 3324, taken from one of the steers killed today.

The menu for us is the same taco salad the slaughter crew ate. I serve myself; and though I'm not in the mood for meat, I add some to my plate. I want to see how I feel eating it.

"Eating meat, I see," Jim says with a smile.

"That means the kill floor didn't derail you," says Mary.

I'm not so sure that's true. Maybe I didn't have a breakdown, but I feel shaken to my core.

I sit down at the picnic table outside and see Mark, the feedlot manager. "It's hard to switch gears, from in there to out here," he says.

I take a bite of my taco salad. The meat is silky and chewy. I force myself to swallow. I take two more bites. Then I stop. It's all too fresh in my mind. At this moment, eating meat feels obscene.

• • •

Mary and I pile into a four-wheeler to see some newborn calves. "I want you to see this part, too," she says, "not just death, but life."

We drive a ways, to a field where we see dozens of calf heifers—cows that have given birth for the first time—with their newborns. Calves just a few days old already have their ear tags. They suckle at their moms' udders. We spot a calf born earlier in the day and drive toward it. The mother moves in protectively. The calf is tiny, black with a white face. It's such a sweet creature. We see another newborn, a Hereford, with shiny russet fur.

The jeep bounces, and I feel something in my pocket stick at me. I pull it out. It's 3324's ear tag. I cradle it in my hand as we drive around.

We head back toward the road. I take one more look at the heifers and their young. The mothers eat quietly while the calves nuzzle and suck. In the distance, the aspens, weeping spruce, and ponderosa pine stand tall against the gentle slopes of the Siskiyous.

• • •

Chopped Cucumber Salad with Grilled Flank Steak and Lemon-Dill Vinaigrette

Serves 6

Meat (if using):
¼ cup soy sauce
2 tablespoons lime juice
3 cloves garlic, crushed
1½ pounds flank steak, trimmed
2 tablespoons olive oil for skillet

Salad:
8 cups cucumbers (about 2 pounds), peeled, seeded, and
    chopped
½ small red onion, peeled and thinly sliced
2 red peppers, diced
1 cup Italian parsley, finely chopped
⅔ cup crumbled blue cheese (optional, especially good if
    not using meat)

Vinaigrette:
⅓ cup extra virgin olive oil
¼ cup fresh lemon juice
2 tablespoons chopped fresh dill
1½ teaspoons honey
Salt and pepper to taste

Mix soy sauce, lime juice, and garlic. Place meat in glass dish and cover with marinade. Cover and let meat sit at least 20 minutes in refrigerator.

Prepare grill or heavy cast-iron skillet over high heat. If using skillet, heat 2 tablespoons olive oil, then add meat.

If grilling, preheat grill to appropriate temperature. (For gas grill, preheat for about ten minutes. For charcoal grill, coals should be glowing red, with top coals an ash gray.) Make sure grill rack is scraped clean. Place meat directly on grill.

Cook meat about 4–6 minutes on each side, making sure it's still pink in the middle. Remove to cutting board. Let stand 20 minutes. Cut into thin slices diagonally across the grain, then cut again into ½-inch pieces.

Combine salad ingredients in large bowl. If using meat or cheese, add to bowl. Whisk together vinaigrette ingredients, pour vinaigrette over salad, and mix well. Serve.

Chapter 11

HOME

The season is changing. You can see it in the light. I have a view of the Hudson River from my window in the B&B in Nyack, New York, where I'm staying. A wind blows, and a shower of golden leaves tumbles from a nearby tree. They dance in semicircles until they reach the ground.

Was this place always so beautiful? I was so eager to leave that, if it was, I didn't notice.

I was born just ten miles from this house. I've always felt a tug to return. I'm here, where my life started, to try to make peace with old ghosts. If I do that, I'm hoping, I can also make peace with the food.

It's a lot to accomplish. I've got a week.

"Unlimited mileage," I tell the man behind the car-rental counter. "And a GPS system, too." I know this turf, but a lot has changed, and I want backup.

I'm headed to the Orchards of Concklin in Pomona, where my mother and I would go, on rare but happy occasions, to buy apples. I'm amazed there are any farms left. In the '60s, when I was born, there were still more than a hundred farms covering about 10,000 acres in Rockland County. Today, there are only a few. This place is one of the only farms from my childhood still standing.

I input the address, and the GPS tells me to get on the Garden State Parkway. I ignore it. I vaguely remember the local streets, and I want to drive them to see how time has changed the place. I head west on Route 59, past stretches of forgettable strip malls. I turn north on Route 45 and pass through the town of Spring Valley, which is run-down and forlorn. The day is warm. I open my window, and a breeze hits my face.

I drive on to Pomona, pull into the farm's parking lot, and then walk into its storefront. The clerk tells me that the owner, Linda Concklin, is in the back office. I head through plastic flapping curtains; enter an old, wooden loft area; and call her name. She comes down a steep flight of steps from her second-floor office and, after a brisk handshake, says, "Let's go to the orchards."

She tells me her family came here from England in the 1630s and settled first in Salem, Massachusetts. Eventually they made their way to Rockland County, establishing this farm in 1712. *Three hundred years is a long time,* I think, as Linda tells me about the apples she grows—Pink Ladies, Macintoshes, Northern Spies, Red and Golden Delicious, Honeycrisps, and other varieties. On a nearby tree, I see one of my all-time favorite varieties—Macouns, which I can't get out West. I grab one and take a bite: its tangy, hard, white flesh is as wonderful as I remember.

She shows me a young orchard where people can pick their own apples. "The revenue from this is what keeps the farm going," she says. "We're not really selling fruit, we're selling entertainment."

Maybe, but it's entertainment that still has a connection to the earth. Though most of the farms in Rockland

County were gone by the time I was a child, the few memories I did have of visiting them made me happy.

I know that Linda has a son, and her brother has two children. As we walk back toward the barn, I ask if the farm will continue.

"This place continues only on the strength of our backs," she says with a shrug. "We'll just have to see. But as long as we're here, we will take care of this land."

I'm not sure what to say. As I leave, I thank her for keeping this place running. I'm grateful that this link to my past is still here, but I know that's only because Linda and her family are willing to do the hard work it takes to run it.

• • •

I head seven miles or so on back roads to Nyack, where I'm meeting Craig Long for coffee at a Dunkin' Donuts on Route 59. Craig is the historian for Ramapo Township, which encompasses much of Rockland County.

I want to understand why, during my childhood, farms disappeared from Rockland. He buys me a cup of coffee, and we sit down at a table. "There's your answer," he says, pointing out the window to the New York State Thruway. "That, and the Tappan Zee Bridge," he says, referring to the bridge that connects Rockland with Westchester County across the Hudson, the same bridge I can see from the window of my room at the B&B.

"Both were built in the 1950s," Craig says, "bringing surges of population to Rockland County. People needed homes. Many of the farmers realized that money was in real estate, not farming; so they sold their farms. The land got chopped up into suburban subdivisions."

I sip the strong coffee, listening to the thrum of thruway traffic from beyond the window.

"Will farming ever come back?" I ask.

Craig shrugs. "Bringing back farmland here will be tough. There's just not a lot of land available.

"Still," he adds, "people today see just how serious things are, and that if we don't change the way we eat and live as a society, we could be in trouble. There are people who understand this here, and are working to change things."

Joan Gussow is one such person. I first learned about Joan, an adjunct professor in the nutrition education department at Columbia University, when I read her book *This Organic Life*. It inspired me to think more deeply about sustainable agriculture and the politics of food production and distribution. She is active in trying to bring farming back to Rockland County.

Joan's garden in Piermont, just a few miles from Nyack, lies on the banks of the Hudson River. I ring her bell, and we head directly out back.

She shows me her pear and apple trees and garden beds filled with basil, chard, peppers, artichokes, and dozens of other vegetables and herbs. It's impressive, but it can't be easy. The county's rocky soil makes it difficult to farm. Joan acknowledges the challenges. "It's hard to grow food on a riverbank," she says. "It's a giant wind tunnel. And, too often, the river floods my garden."

I ask her why she perseveres, beyond the obvious delight of eating garden-fresh food. "We live in such a cynical world, where people are not what they seem," she replies. "It matters to my students that I live what I teach."

Though she lives only a dozen or so miles from where I grew up, the world she has created here is vastly different. She gets most of her food from her garden, successfully feeding herself using the same soil that left me feeling hungry all the time.

• • •

A storm arrives overnight. Outside my window, the wind is blowing hard; and the Hudson is choppy.

Carolla Dost, who owns the Riverview Bed & Breakfast, where I'm staying, whips up a delicious omelet with fresh herbs from her garden. Her two Pomeranians, Honey and Buttons, sit patiently at my feet, waiting for handouts. Unable to resist their adorable faces, I give each of them a piece.

Outside, the air is chilly. I head toward Pomona to visit Alexandra Spadea and her husband, John McDowell, of Camp Hill Farm, Rockland County's first Community Supported Agriculture farm. I have to swerve to avoid downed branches and the occasional tree.

When I first contacted Alex, her warmth was palpable, even over e-mail. So when I pull in and she comes to greet me, I don't hesitate to throw my arms around her. She laughs and hugs me back.

We walk over to a round picnic table that sits next to the house, and Alex introduces me to John, as well as to Dave Gutierrez, who works with them. We sit down, and Alex brings me a cup of strong coffee spiked with heavy cream.

Camp Hill feeds 37 families from just one acre of land. The farm is biodynamic, a system of sustainable agriculture developed by Rudolf Steiner, the late-19th-century philosopher who founded the Anthroposophy spiritual movement and left a strong imprint on this part of the country. Steiner viewed all life forms—animals, plants, humans, the earth itself—as interconnected, with every part needing to be healthy for the whole to thrive.

"Every day, people visit who want to convert their small land into a garden," John says. "The suburbs have been left out of farming; but in Rockland, that's mostly all that's left. So we need to work with what we've got and stop paving our way into annihilation."

John and Alex founded Camp Hill Farm in 2005. Realizing that a small farm needed the support of its community, in 2007 they created the Rockland Farm Alliance, an organization to facilitate sustainable agriculture in the county. "A farmer at an early meeting told us that farming in Rockland was dead," said John. "We're not hearing that anymore." At their first big community outreach meeting, more than 250 people showed up.

As we talk, I hear a quack in the distance. Alex walks over to a nearby field and opens a gate. A minute later, a duck named Rachel waddles up and joins us at the table.

"She thinks she's a dog," I say.

"She is a dog," says Alex, "except she's a duck."

Farming is a noble profession, but it doesn't pay well, and so neither Alex nor John has quit his day job. Alex teaches eurythmy, a kind of dance and movement therapy created by Steiner; and John is a composer and a pianist who scored the 2004 film *Born into Brothels,* which won an Academy Award for Best Documentary Feature.

"Music and farming seems like an inspired combination," I say to John.

He nods. "Music is ethereal, but the earth is physical," he says. "They balance and inform each other."

Alex invites me to walk around. Rachel the duck joins us.

We enter a small, round garden. "This is where Camp Hill Farm started," she says. She shows me amaranth, salvia, nasturtiums, echinacea, wormwood, valerian, stinging nettles, and yarrow, planted in concentric circles. All of these plants are used in biodynamic preparations to help nourish the soil.

"I grew up in a Waldorf school in Germany," she says, referring to the experiential-based educational system Steiner founded in 1919. "After I studied and taught eurythmy and had a child and John and I grew a garden, I realized I had a deep connection to the earth—she is the one who holds us, who receives us, and who cares for us. I started to grow food, and the earth was kind, and she gave back."

We move on to the larger field behind the house with Rachel at our side. Alex shows me African marigolds, Russian kale, bush beans, winter rye, sunflowers, carrots, beets, peppers, mustard greens, leeks, and arugula. As we walk in the fields, a young woman comes to pick up her farm basket. Alex goes to greet her and I follow. The woman looks at the contents of her basket and seems a little intimidated. "What's this?" she asks, holding up a springy sheaf of greens.

"That's kale," Alex says, and gives her some simple instructions for how to cook it. The woman smiles, still looking uncertain, then takes her basket and leaves.

We head back to the table. John and Alex's five-year-old daughter, Luna, has just returned from her first day of school. Alex scoops her up in her arms. "Against all odds we're still here," she says. "We lease this land, month to month; and we're now going on ten years."

The air is cool. I wrap myself in my sweater and look around. The land is dotted with the brilliant red-and-gold leaves of sugar maples. A giant spruce stands guard in the distance, like a sentry.

I tell Alex that this place touches something old and deep in me. "Do you feel it, too?" I ask as she walks me to my car to say good-bye.

"I feel it strongest when I work the land and see how the community is nourished by it," she says. "And when that happens, it's as if the spirits whisper to us. Camp Hill Farm is our answer to their call."

• • •

The next morning I make my way to my childhood home.

Two weeks earlier, I sent a letter to the current residents: "To Whom This May Concern . . ." I explained that I was writing a book and that I'd like to visit, adding that if they didn't want me to, I'd understand.

I drive into the development with its modest split-level homes. My old house sits on a small hill. It's still pretty. The two boulders my mother put in when she landscaped our house are there. Were they always so small? The weeping willow still weeps, but the rhododendron bushes from the front are gone, as are the lilac bushes, now replaced with some kind of hedge. I walk up to the door and ring the bell.

A woman opens the door a tiny crack. I say hello and tell her who I am. Yes, she says, she got my letter. "But I don't know you," she says, with a lilting island accent. "I'm sorry. You're a complete stranger. I can't let you in. I hope you understand."

I tell her I do; all the while taking surreptitious looks past her. I see the stairs that lead up to the living room and down to the den. The burnt-orange shag rug has been replaced by beige carpet, but I can't see much more than that.

"Would you mind if I walked around the property?" I ask. She smiles and says that would be fine, then closes the door with a quiet click.

I walk back down to the front lawn. Here is where I made snow angels in the winter and watched stars on warm summer nights. I look up at the house. There's the kitchen window, the site of endless olive forays, Swanson TV dinners consumed in front of *I Dream of Jeannie* and *Gilligan's Island,* and the exploding flan.

The front door suddenly opens. The woman and a man I assume is her husband walk out. Even though I have her permission, I feel like I'm lurking. "Thank you for letting me walk around your yard," I tell them.

The man smiles and says, "I understand. It's very sentimental." I smile back. He's kind but wrong; I am feeling, instead, oddly detached.

They say good-bye, get into their car, and drive off.

Alone now, I stand in front of my old house. I have the urge to peer through the windows but I don't. I head back down the driveway toward my rental car.

Glancing back at my old bedroom window, I remember how, as a young girl, I couldn't find the courage to write a book and think how grateful I am to write this one now. Sometimes there are promises you make to yourself that you have to keep, because if you didn't, life would be too dispiriting.

I pause and say a silent good-bye to this house, grateful that I never gave up on the young girl who wanted more.

• • •

After I leave my old house, I head toward Hungry Hollow Road. It's just one mile away; but growing up, it felt like another world. I used to walk down this winding, tree-lined street and see glass jars filled with beans and grains sitting on the sills of kitchen windows. Those jars seemed so mysterious they might as well have lived in a magician's workshop. It took me a few decades and a move across the country to realize that the key to their transformation was simply water and time.

Hungry Hollow Road is home to the Threefold Educational Center, whose mission is to continue the teachings of Rudolf Steiner. As a child, I didn't know about this connection, only that this land seemed different and interesting. Even the street's name drew me to it. The property was purchased in 1926 by some of Steiner's students, beginning the spread of Steiner's influence in Rockland County. Today, its 140 acres are home to various enterprises, including the Pfeiffer Center for Biodynamics and the Environment, which includes an education-and-demonstration garden. That's where I'm going now.

I'm greeted by the center's director, Mac Mead, who has worked in the Threefold community for more than 30 years. We walk over to the demonstration garden, which is thought to be the oldest biodynamic garden in the country; and Mac shows me some of the many crops he grows, including buckwheat, amaranth, sunflowers, quince, fennel, winter squash, borage, beets, bell peppers, scotch thistle, anise hyssop, and mullein. I pluck a pepper off the vine and bite. It is crunchy and bursting with vitality.

Mac tells me that Steiner believed that human beings and the natural world evolve together. "In order
to be nourished, you have to eat food that comes from
nourished soil," he says. "If the plants get what they
need, so do we."

He asks me if I'd like to see the oldest section of the
community. We get in my car and drive down a bumpy
dirt road, heading toward Duryea Farm. As my eyes take
in acres of apple orchards and some grazing sheep and
cows, Mac tells me the farm was established in 1883. We
park near an old brown barn. It is so quiet here. Inside,
the hay bales smell to me like freshly baked bread. Faded
pictures of old farmers, probably from the original farm,
hang on a wall.

I see an old staircase and head toward it. Mac tells me
to be careful, then waits as I explore. I climb up into a
loft filled with more hay bales. In the late-afternoon light
that streams through a large window, I can see whorls of
dust. I walk up to the window and look through. I know
my childhood home is just over the hills, but I still find
that hard to believe.

• • •

Before I return home, Robyn and I go to the cem-
etery in New Jersey where our father is buried. We look
at the map we got when he died, now yellowed with age,
and find his plot. We hold hands as we walk toward his
grave.

We stand there, not saying much. Though the graves
are maintained, litter blows around and gets caught in
the hedge that sits in front of his and his parents' graves.

I find an old beer can, some paper, a candy wrapper, and a golf ball. I clean up all the junk and put it in a bag to throw away.

Everything about this day is gray—the sky, the bare plants, the headstones. My eyes crave color. I see a couple of berries on a nearby tree, pluck a few, and place them on the graves' footstones. "May you be happy," I say to my father, "wherever you are."

I place my hand on the headstone and say good-bye.

I head to the car, glancing back one more time. The red berries look beautiful against the gray stone.

• • •

Black Bean Soup with Sherry and Herbs

Serves 8

2 cups dry black beans, picked over for stones
1–2 tablespoons olive oil (depending on whether
    pancetta is used)
4 ounces diced pancetta (optional)
1 cup diced onions (about 1 small onion)
1 cup diced carrots (about 2 carrots)
1 cup chopped celery (about 2 stalks)
2 cloves garlic, minced (about 2 teaspoons)
2 teaspoons dried thyme
2 ounces dry sherry
Salt and pepper to taste

Place beans in heavy pot with two quarts water and bring to a boil. Turn heat to low and cook 1 hour. Drain beans and set aside. Rinse pot.

If using pancetta, heat 1 tablespoon olive oil in the same pot over medium-high heat and cook pancetta 7–9 minutes or until cooked through and crispy. Remove pancetta with slotted spoon. Leave two tablespoons of fat in the pot and discard the rest. If not using pancetta, heat 2 tablespoons olive oil in the pot.

Add onions, carrots, celery, garlic, and thyme. Cook about 5 minutes or until vegetables begin to soften. Add beans and 8 cups water. Bring to a boil, then cook, covered, on low heat 3–4 hours.

If using pancetta, return pancetta to pot. Puree if you prefer a smooth soup. Add sherry and stir. Salt and pepper to taste. Makes 14 cups.

Part III

Transformation

As I dig for wild orchids in the autumn fields,
It is the deeply-bedded root that I desire,
Not the flower.

— Izumi Shikibu

The breeze at dawn has secrets to tell you.
Don't go back to sleep.
You must ask for what you really want.
Don't go back to sleep.
People are going back and forth across the doorsill
where the two worlds touch.
The door is round and open.
Don't go back to sleep.

— RUMI

Chapter 12

NO FOOD

As far as I've gone on this journey, I haven't fundamentally changed. I imagined that by some mysterious process, nature would heal me. I thought that returning to my childhood haunts and coming to terms with my memories would somehow liberate me. But neither has.

I didn't think it would be this hard. I'm angry and a little freaked out. What secret am I missing? What link in the chain have I overlooked?

I've always counted on the power of my intellect to get me where I want to go. It usually has, but not here. Understanding counts, but it doesn't equal transformation.

I know that willpower is important; and in the really difficult aspects of my life, I've applied it firmly, all or nothing. I quit smoking cigarettes. Why can't I just summon the power of my will and conquer my problems? Perhaps I could, but I don't want that kind of victory. I'm looking for balance and peace—and going to war with my body doesn't feel like it will get me there.

I feel backed against a wall. And I'm seeing some truths that hurt. I feel fat. I feel invisible. My knees ache. My ankles hurt. I'm turning 50. I'm setting the stage for the second half of my life, and I don't like what I see.

• • •

"You'll fast for three days," Scott Blossom tells me. We are sitting in the garden of his Northern California home. Blossom teaches me yoga. He's also a holistic healer who incorporates Ayurveda in his work. I've chosen my next step, and I'm turning to him for guidance.

I've run from hunger my whole life, and now I'm going to turn and face it. But does it really have to be for three full days?

I begin to bargain. "Two," I say. "Two is good."

"No," he says, "three. Three is what you need to wrestle with issues deeper than the physical manifestation of hunger."

"Like what?" I ask.

"Like how it feels to get off autopilot," he says. "And how to identify real hunger instead of hunger out of habit."

"This is the beginning of real change," he tells me. "Transformation without some basic reconstruction of the habit patterns is unwise." *Kind of like remodeling a home that's built on a crumbling foundation,* I think—it may look great, but one day it will probably fall down.

"I'm afraid of my hunger," I tell him, "afraid of how I'll respond."

"Take your hunger on," he says. "It will make you wide awake. Three days is short. If you get through this, you might crack your code; and your contract with food will change.

"The real work is to let whatever arises arise, and to do so without snuffing it out with food. And when you do," he adds, "you'll notice that things pass and that maybe you're not who you think you are."

• • •

Blossom suggests that during my fast I drink a strained vegetable broth. He tells me this is better for me than just water, because the vitamins and minerals in the broth will help keep me steady.

The day before I begin, I go to the market and buy heaps of beets, potatoes, carrots, string beans, celery, onions, garlic, and parsley. I get home, scrub and peel the root vegetables, and add the peels to a large stockpot filled with water. I wash and cut the string beans, chop the onion, take the top off an entire head of garlic, and throw all this into the pot along with a bunch of parsley. I bring the concoction to a boil, let it simmer for an hour, and then strain it. The beet peels have made the broth a beautiful, light claret color.

Later that evening, as I'm preparing dinner, I notice a small container of olives in the refrigerator. In a kind of prophylactic binge, I eat them all, telling myself it's better they're out of the way so I won't be tempted tomorrow. I sit down with my family and eat a good-sized portion of eggplant parmesan; and though I'm no longer hungry, I take another helping. "The last supper," I joke as I take my final bite.

• • •

It's early morning. I heat up some broth and take it outside onto the deck. It's an Indian-summer day, and I'm grateful for the mildness of the weather. The wind gently blows the steam off the top of my mug.

I take a sip. It's a little watery; but I can still taste the innate sweetness of the carrots, onions, and beets.

As the morning moves on, my stomach starts to rumble. It feels like a dull ache. Over the next hour, it recedes, then returns, stronger this time. Then it recedes again, like a tide moving toward and away from the shore.

The front page of the *New York Times* food section sits on the dining-room table. It features luscious foods to serve on Rosh Hashanah, the beginning of the Jewish New Year, which starts in two days. I flip the paper over and walk away.

Lunchtime. I heat some broth and drink slowly, making it last as long as possible. The waves of hunger move in and out. I try to watch the sensations and let them go.

It's now 4 P.M. Though the broth keeps me steady and grounded, I feel an internal lightness that is unfamiliar. A friend of mine who practices yoga and is a dancer once told me she loves the sensation of being lighter than air. I was shocked. I couldn't imagine desiring that. When I was young, I ate more than I needed, hoping that my solidity would keep me grounded, tethered to the earth. Eventually, overeating became a habit. Though it long ago stopped serving me, it's still a hard habit to break.

I need to get out of the kitchen and away from food. I head to the garden and begin pulling out dead acanthus. The plants, which bloom in spring, are now shriveled and brown. I cut down the giant flower stalks, gather up the crunchy leaves, and put them in the compost bin. I have energy to burn, and I start ripping the plants out of the ground. The pile of dead leaves grows higher, and I begin to sweat. *I'm not eating. I want some food. I'm not eating. I'm angry. Keep gardening. I want to eat. I can't. Oh yeah? Says who? Fuck you.*

It's not even been a full day, and my inner rebel has already emerged. I know her well—she's the same person who led a revolt (of one) on the girls' playground at my elementary school because the girls' equipment was inferior to the boys'. The same inner rebel who recoils from the word "diet." (*Who the hell are you to tell me what to eat?*) Forty years later, she's alive and kicking.

I pull more acanthus plants until sweat is pouring down my back.

I come back into the house and wash up. Scott has taken the boys out for Mexican food, so I won't be tempted with the smells of home cooking. I spy a bag of pumpkin seeds on the counter and almost grab a few, then catch myself.

I want a distraction. I go into my office and start trolling Websites for shoes. I see a pair of divine red ankle-straps and consider buying them, until I realize I'm just trading one obsession for another.

I pass on the shoes but go to the Three Stone Hearth Website to check out this week's offerings. The kitchen, based in Berkeley, serves prepared organic meals that you can order in advance and then pick up. I read the online menu: Roasted Tomato & Red Pepper Yogurt Cream with Scallions, Chicken Gumbo with Rice, Mocha Coconut Cream Mousse. Ummmm, mousse—creamy, velvety mousse. I place an order for pickup the following week.

6 P.M. It's time for what now passes for dinner. I heat my broth and return to the deck to drink it. The sun is low in the sky. The air is warm and still. I begin to fantasize about my first meal, still more than 48 hours away. I've already planned it: sautéed tofu with Thai basil.

The boys come home from dinner. Soon they wash up and are in bed. I often eat at night; but if I can't eat now, what else should I do? I go down to my library and notice an old volume of Nancy Drew on a shelf. I loved Nancy Drew as a kid. I grab the book and begin to read. Not much has changed in River Heights in 40 years. Nancy still has "titian" hair and drives a blue roadster. Hannah Gruen, the housekeeper, still begs Nancy to take extreme caution. The bad guys are "bewhiskered," have greasy hair, and use knockout spray; Bess, one of Nancy's best friends, is still "plump"; and George, Bess's cousin, still chides Bess about her weight. Nancy and her father, the famous criminal lawyer Carson Drew, still sit down to dinner and eat Hannah's delicious meatloaf and strawberry chiffon cake.

An hour passes and I've already read through most of the slight book. Though the writing is clunky and formulaic, I take solace in it. Reading these books made me so happy as a kid, and I'm just as happy to read one now.

I make some licorice tea and take it out to the deck. Venus is huge, glittering in the sky. I'm hungry, but not yet suffering. Maybe some suffering is optional. Maybe there is a choice.

I get ready for bed. I do feel a rare lightness in my body, which makes me feel vulnerable. Tears lie close to the surface.

I recently received a kind of deep-tissue bodywork known as Rolfing. While on the table, I asked Michael Salveson, the insightful man I see for this work, why it's so hard to change eating habits.

"Change is not a matter of willpower," he said. "It's a matter of presence." He told me to study hunger. "If you sit with it long enough, it often moves from your stomach to your heart. It's a kind of longing."

It is. I can feel it in my chest. I see a book of Rumi poems on my nightstand, reach over, and open it. My eyes fall upon the poem "The Seed Market":

You've been fearful
of being absorbed in the ground,
or drawn up by the air.

Now, your waterbead lets go
and drops into the ocean,
where it came from.

It no longer has the form it had,
but it's still water.
The essence is the same.

This giving up is not a repenting.
It's a deep honoring of yourself . . .

As I drift off to sleep, I realize I'm not repenting by giving up food for three days; I'm honoring myself by letting what I've kept hidden under endless mounds of food finally see the light of day.

• • •

Sunrise. The first rays of light enter our bedroom. Something's different. It's my body; it's so quiet. I'm not digesting or chewing or swallowing. There's no food in my gut to take that long journey through my digestive tract.

I notice something else. My breathing has changed. I have a habit left over from childhood of holding my breath after I inhale—as if to hang on to each lungful of air. Today, my breathing is just in and out, in and out.

After the kids leave for school and I drink my morning broth, I get dressed and head up the road to see my friend Chandra Easton, a Tibetan scholar and yoga teacher, who is Scott Blossom's wife. She is studying a practice known as Feeding Your Demons. Developed by the Buddhist teacher Tsultrim Allione, Feeding Your Demons is based on an ancient Tibetan practice of Chöd, which means "cutting through." I thought a fast would be an auspicious time to meet some of the demons I try to subdue with food.

Chandra makes me a cup of tea, then invites me to sit on a cushion on the floor. Instructing me to close my eyes, she begins asking me a series of questions and says I should tell her the first things that come to mind.

"What demon do you want to work with?"

Self-importance.

"Does it have a feeling? A color? A texture?"

It's an ache—a bone-colored string with lots of little knots spaced evenly apart.

"Where is it held in your body?"

In my right abdomen. It's curved—it moves up between my breasts and ends at my heart.

"What does it look like now?"

The string is changing. It's aging, getting older. I see immense sadness. Now it's changing again. It's become a kind of human form, with graying skin. Now the form starts to cave in on her. She holds herself tighter, trying to stop herself from disappearing, but can't. Her bones begin to disintegrate and turn to dust. The wind picks the dust up, and it starts to fly away.

"What does the demon want?"

Love.

"What does it need?"

Recognition and acceptance.

"When its needs are met, it will feel . . ."
Light and free.

The next step in the process is to feed the demon some sweet, nourishing nectar that has the qualities of my last answer. I feed it lightness and freedom. Chandra asks me how the demon is receiving it.

"She's greedy," I say, "and endlessly thirsty." The demon's birdlike, with a stretched neck and open beak. I briefly see my mother's face before it changes again. Is my mother hungry? I think she is. I made her soup recently, with barley, lamb, and carrots. She lapped up every morsel, my mother, who says she's not interested in food.

The demon-bird is a Hungry Ghost, the Buddhist image of a creature that can never be satisfied. This bird has a tiny mouth, a bottomless stomach, and an endless appetite. The bird will never be satisfied by food. The bird needs love. The bird needs recognition and acceptance.

Chandra tells me to look for my ally, the figure that will help and protect me through my demon journey. I tell her I don't see a figure, but I feel her strong and stable presence; she's an adult in the fullest sense of the word.

"What is her gift to you?"

"Her gift," I say, as I begin to cry, "is to help me bear witness to my shortcomings and sadness, without getting submerged."

• • •

Dinnertime. Scott is kind and once again takes the boys out so I don't have to smell cooked food. I drink my broth.

I know my first meal is not for another 24 hours, but I begin anyway. I put on a pot of brown rice. I wash the green beans, snip the ends off, and cut them on a diagonal. I rinse the shiitakes, take off the bottom of each stem, and slice them thinly. I wash the basil and pat it dry. Should I cut it into a chiffonade? This last step should wait; the basil will wilt before I can use it. But I do it anyway. I must be prepared.

Prepared for what? Prepared to eat at the very moment I'm allowed to because I'm starving? But I'm not, in fact, starving. Why am I preparing for a calamity that may never arise? How much of my eating is preparation for some imagined imminent disaster?

I feel lightheaded, but I'm okay. I've had a picture of how this fast would go. It included deprivation, anger, and images of pacing the floor like some caged beast. None of that has happened. What other pictures do I hold on to that aren't real?

I wash my bowl and head upstairs. I take out another Nancy Drew. I pass the next hour reading, until suddenly I feel a wrenching hunger in my gut. This is no gentle wave lapping upon my shore. It's a stab, and it is direct and pitiless. I put Nancy aside and sit up. Here it comes again. Shit. I rub my stomach, trying to massage it out.

It's like I'm in an elevator that's just dropped a few floors. I start feeling anxious and begin to sweat, my equanimity swept away. I usually plug my anxiety with food. But I am here to be with hunger. So I just sit with it.

My anxiety morphs into sadness. I mourn the creeping invisibility of middle age and the gradual thickening of my body. I mourn the loss of my youthful beauty and all the time I wasted not seeing just how beautiful I was. All because I was never thin enough.

Salami. I want salami. And not just any salami; but the Fra' Mani handcrafted salami created by Paul

Bertolli, former chef of Chez Panisse. And not just any of his salamis but his Salame Nostrano, a chewy, perfect blend of pork, salt, and spice.

I start to salivate. Drool, really. My sadness has moved on and has morphed again, this time into a full-blown, sky-high craving. *Just read,* I tell myself. It will go away. I try to go back to Nancy. She's tapping another wall to see if it's hollow, but I can't concentrate with the images of salami parading through my brain.

What else can satisfy me that doesn't involve eating? I pace the floor. Don't consume—create. I pick up my guitar, then put it down. I can't get this salami out of my mind.

If I hadn't been on a fast, if I hadn't made a commitment to seeing this through, I'm not sure that I could withstand this hunger. But I made a commitment, so here I am.

A line from another Rumi poem comes to me:

> *Move within,*
> *but don't move the way fear makes you move.*

Five minutes pass, then ten minutes, and then fifteen. I go back to reading. I'm fidgety. I go downstairs to wash dishes. I go back upstairs, read some more; and before I know it, a half hour has gone by, and Nancy has solved another mystery.

I'm astonished. My craving has moved on. It's true what Buddhism and other wisdom traditions say—things pass. Everything changes. Nothing stays the same.

Desires are deceptive. We think that if we fill them, we'll be satisfied. But isn't it true that if you satisfy one desire, another one will inevitably arise?

Today, the salami showed me these truths in action.

• • •

Morning of the third day. I get out of bed and do some light stretching. My body feels more spacious than usual. I head downstairs and heat up more broth. This time, I actually gag on it.

Tonight is Rosh Hashanah, the start of the Jewish New Year and the beginning of the ten-day period known as the Days of Awe. I decide spontaneously to cook my family a classic holiday dinner. I hadn't planned on it, because I've been so focused on my fast, but I want to. I will still eat my much-anticipated Thai basil tofu dish, but I will also make some roast chicken and potatoes for my family.

I drive to the market. Why am I planning a multi-course dinner when I haven't eaten any food for days? It's true that cooking food is one way I nurture my family. It's also true that food is so central to my life that even when I'm fasting, I can't seem to drag myself away from it.

I get home and throw myself into a cooking frenzy. I make a honey soy glaze, brush it over the chicken, and pop it all in the oven. I peel the potatoes, cut them into wedges, mix them with olive oil and sea salt, and put them in to roast. I mince the garlic for the string beans. All the ingredients for the stir-fry are ready to go. Dinner in an hour—my first food in three days.

I see a bag of salted, roasted walnuts on the counter. I reach for them. They look so delicious. Does an hour really matter?

Yes, it does. I walk away.

I set the table. On it I place candles, a bottle of wine, and a round challah I bought from a bakery. I put out water glasses. I ask the boys to go to the garden and pick a bouquet for the table.

Fifteen minutes to go. The smell of food fills the kitchen. I start to salivate. I put the stir-fry on. The garlic, lemongrass, and green beans hit the pan with a sizzle and fill the air with a spicy citrus scent. I see a pomegranate sitting on the counter and decide to serve it, too—such a gorgeous, autumnal fruit.

The boys come back with some pink and red geraniums, which I put in a vase.

Five minutes to go. I put a trivet on the table and place the hot chicken pan on it. I serve the potato wedges in a bowl. I put the stir-fry into another bowl and bring it to the table. Scott pours wine for us and grape juice for the boys. Finally, we are ready.

I light the candles, cover my eyes, and say the prayer. Scott says the blessing over the wine. The boys say the blessing over the bread. I tell them how grateful I am that we are a family.

I serve them chicken, potatoes, and vegetables. Then I serve myself a small wedge of pomegranate.

The seeds, or arils, are garnet red, transparent and luminous. I pop one in my mouth, which receives it with a pucker. They are so sour that I cannot eat more than one at a time, and each one demands time and attention. This, I'm sure, is the result of my fast—every part of me has slowed down.

I serve myself some stir-fry. I dig in, making sure my spoon gets everything the dish has to offer—lemongrass, string beans, and tofu. I notice the crunch of the beans, then the salt of the sauté. The dish is tasty, and I enjoy my first bite. But I'm disappointed. I expected something more, well, dazzling. The food is good, but the picture in my mind was so much better. I eat a little more, then stop. My stomach has shrunk over the last few days, and I'm already full. I sit with my family until they are finished.

After dinner, I head to Tilden Park to perform a ritual known as *tashlich,* which means "casting off." It's a ceremony that's done between Rosh Hashanah and Yom Kippur in which you toss a piece of bread into water and say a prayer to cast off your sins.

I'm not much for the idea of sin, but I'm all for letting go of what is no longer necessary. I hike out to Jewel Lake and stand by the water's edge. Some ducks swim by while a dragonfly swoops down and lands on a nearby rock. *I'm ready for change,* I say as I throw a piece of bread in the water. *I'm ready to be lighter, freer in body and spirit.* I throw another piece of bread in the water. *I'm ready to have food find its proper place in my world and not be my world.* I throw another piece. *I want to be comfortable in my own skin.*

I take the last few pieces of bread, toss them in the water, and watch them float away.

· · ·

Fasting Broth

3 pounds each, organic beets, potatoes, and carrots
1 bunch parsley
1 pound green beans
1 onion, peeled and cut into quarters
1 head garlic, top cut off
1 bunch celery, cleaned and very coarsely chopped

Scrub and peel beets, potatoes, and carrots. Save the peels (about 6 packed cups) and reserve the vegetables for another use.

Place peels and remaining ingredients in large stockpot with 4 quarts water. Bring to a boil over high heat, then reduce heat to medium-low and simmer for at least an hour. Remove all vegetables and peels. Drink broth for as long as you choose to fast and freeze leftovers for later use. Makes about 10 cups.

Chapter 13

THE YOGA OF FOOD

It's 4 A.M. and dark. The sun won't rise for another two hours. It's still the dreaming hour as I get out of bed, put on my yoga clothes, and head downstairs to my mat.

Hands in prayer position, I begin—*Surya Namaskar,* Salute to the Sun. I reach my arms up to the sky, then down to the ground in a standing forward bend. Stepping back with my legs, I move into Downward Dog. Lowering my body parallel to the floor, I lift my head and reach my chest forward in Upward Dog. Back into Downward Dog. I move through the sequence again and again.

I don't usually do yoga at 4 in the morning, but this is the practice Scott Blossom, one of my yoga teachers, gave me. I've studied yoga for over 15 years; and more than any other practice, yoga helps me see the world and myself more clearly.

I asked Blossom to give me a sequence I could do at home that would help me to "unwind" my *samskaras,* the yogic concept of habits and patterns that become etched into the nervous system. Samskaras act like the grooves a wheel makes in a muddy road—the more the wheel spins in that groove, the deeper the groove gets, and the more difficult it is for the wheel to break free of it. When we continue to act and think in habitual ways, without ever really challenging these patterns, they become a part of us, making it difficult for us to behave or think differently. The only way to get out of the rut is through diligent practice and attention.

When I asked Blossom to recommend a practice, he looked at me warily. I knew what he was thinking—that it's hubris to request something that I will only be able to do for a few months before writing about it. And he's right. Liberation never comes that easily.

Maybe that's why he challenged me with a series of demanding poses and told me to do them between 4 and 5 in the morning. When I asked why I couldn't do it at a more civilized hour, he said, "Because the deep work is often done in the dark."

• • •

I imagined that Blossom would give me a practice that functioned metaphorically. If I wanted to cultivate the quality of courage, he'd give me an inversion, like a handstand. If I wanted to let go of my distractibility, he'd give me a balancing posture, like Tree Pose. For my tendency toward greed, he'd give me a pose at which I'm relatively adept, like Half Lotus, and have me pull back to learn restraint. To open my still-armored heart, he'd give me a backbend.

But Blossom doesn't want me to think. He wants me to sweat. He gives me a flow practice, incorporating elements of Shadow Yoga, a form of yoga developed by his teacher, Zhander Remete, to help free the body of energetic blocks. The practice consists of spiraling, circular, and linear movements that integrate the principles common to yoga asanas, martial arts, South Indian dance, and Ayurvedic medicine. I'm not used to this, having trained in the Iyengar system, where you hold poses focusing on precision and alignment. I feel awkward and get winded easily.

Up, down, squat, lunge, twist, forward bend, backbend, lunge, twist. "You have a body that needs to be treated firmly, like a cob house," Blossom said, referring to a building made from clay, sand, water, straw, and earth. "You're strong, but if you don't mix your elements right and build enough fire and heat, you'll turn to mush."

More lunges, more sweat. I'm in unfamiliar terrain. If I could do whatever I wanted, it would be a restorative practice. Drape me over a yoga bolster and retrieve me in an hour.

"No," Blossom said. "You have to build heat. It's fire that will transform you."

His last instruction is to "live in your legs and root your feet. Transformation," he says, "doesn't happen just from the neck up. It happens when your feet are rooted to the earth."

• • •

I call Ana Forrest, my friend and the creator of Forrest Yoga. I've known Ana for years and am often moved by the ferocity of her practice and by her kindness. Ana is a former binge eater and bulimic, so I am especially curious about how she has dealt with her own "food" samskaras.

The simplicity of her answer surprises me. "If I need to make a choice about what I'm going to eat, what I'm going to say, what I'm going to do, I ask myself one question: Does this brighten or dim my spirit? Puking dims my spirit. Bingeing dims my spirit. I simply will not do that anymore."

"What if your spirit tells you to eat salami?" I ask.

"It won't," she says. "There a difference between the voice of spirit and the voice of addiction. There will be a certain dissonance. Something will be off. And your belly will feel tight."

• • •

It's early morning, and I'm lying facedown on my mat with a yoga block under my belly.

Bo Forbes, a psychologist and yoga teacher in Cambridge, Massachusetts, and author of *Yoga for Emotional Balance,* suggested this unusual pose in order to wake up my relationship with my core body. She knows I have a tendency to check out when it comes to my stomach, and lying on a block in this area forces me to pay attention. She had me do the same pose a few years ago when I studied with her in Boston. Back then I barely lasted ten seconds; the sensations were too intense. But here I am, two years later, trying again.

The block presses into most of my abdominal organs—my large and small intestines, my liver, my stomach. Bo tells me to engage the *bandhas*—a kind of internal contraction—in this pose. In yoga, there are many bandhas throughout the body; but today I am working with *mula bandha,* or "root lock," a lifting of the muscles of the perineum, and *uddiyana bandha,* or "upward flying lock," which extends from the lower abdomen to the lower ribs. Engaging them in this pose brings greater focus and energy to my abdomen.

It's still an uncomfortable pose, but I'm committed. Ten seconds pass, then twenty. I stay with the sensation for a minute. I feel my pulse throughout my abdominal area, wave after wave of pumping blood.

What I first notice is an ache in my stomach; followed by a sense of extreme tiredness; and then, surprisingly, shyness. If my stomach were outside of my body, she'd be trying to hide. She wants to live in the shadows—to be fed but not seen.

• • •

4:30 A.M. I'm on my mat, doing a pose sequence known as *Vani*, which feels more like dance than yoga. I move my legs into *Garudasana*, or Eagle Pose, a cross-legged squat, arms twisted around each other in front of me. I hold the squat, then switch to the other side and hold the squat again. I repeat this a dozen more times.

I'm surprised that I can actually do the pose, hold it, and then keep repeating it, over and over again. I'm surprised by my strength. I've focused so long on my excess, my weight, the story I tell myself about myself, that I often forget how capable my body is.

This morning I did a pose called *Chaturanga Dandasana*, a kind of push-up, which I've never done before. I made one modification in the placement of my arms and there I was, up and down, up and down. "But I don't do Chaturanga," I would always tell my yoga teachers. Now I do.

My friend Timothy McCall, a medical doctor and author of *Yoga as Medicine*, once told me, "Yoga teaches you not to get lost in your stories. Yoga helps you see clearly and receive the direct experience of yourself. Not the story you make up about yourself, but your true experience of who you are."

I agree. So what happens when you lose the stories you've created about yourself? What replaces them?

"When you develop new samskaras and replace fantasies with clear vision, you're leaving an old order behind," Bo says. "That order may not have been healthy, but it was familiar and comfortable. When you leave it behind, you enter a kind of transition state, a *bardo* in Tibetan terms. Being present in this state requires faith, because you're not sure where you'll land, and fearlessness, because it's so unformed."

She's right. I don't know where I'll land. But the path of yoga feels authentic. And I have faith that the universe has my back.

• • •

A few weeks into my samskara practice, I have a dream:

I'm at some kind of yoga, music, and art conference. On the walls are photos and paintings of sinewy models in yoga poses. The title of the exhibit is "Lethe," which in Greek mythology is one of the rivers of the underworld. Whoever drank from this river was doomed to forget. In one painting, there's a skinny model with black disks all over her body. The disks seem to block the flow of energy in her body. She is so skinny her bones jut out. She seems listless, lifeless even. I wonder what it is she's forgotten?

The scene shifts and my husband, some friends, and I listen to a singer who is performing at the conference.

She is middle-aged, and her voice is beautiful—rich and dusky. I find her inspiring.

When she's finished with her set, she joins us for lunch. There's a pot of jasmine tea on the table, and I pour everyone a cup. As we begin to sip it, my friend asks the singer how her diet's going.

"Diet?" she asks, looking puzzled.

"You've lost weight," my friend continues.

My ears perk up. "You lost weight?" I ask. "Can you tell me what you're eating?"

She nods. "The secret is . . ." She pauses, and with a Mona Lisa smile says, "There is no secret."

And then I wake up.

• • •

The fog is thick outside my window. It's still dark. All I can see are the tops of the conifers peeping out above the blanket of mist.

I begin my practice. I'm bored, and I find myself in the familiar position of starting to bargain with myself. *I can skip it just this once, right?* I ignore that.

I begin my Sun Salutations. I can't stop yawning. I do them anyway.

I see now why Blossom gave me this 4 A.M. practice. He doesn't believe a month of this will change my life, and neither do I. But sticking with it will show me I have the strength and gumption to change my relationship with food.

Arms lifted to the sky. Breathe. Hands to the floor, Downward Dog.

The sun is not up yet, but it will be soon.

Root Fries Tossed with Gremolata

Serves 4

2 pounds root vegetables in whatever combination you like:
    potatoes, sweet potatoes, carrots, yams, rutabagas, and/or
    parsnips
4 tablespoons good-quality olive oil
1 teaspoon Celtic sea salt
2 tablespoons chopped fresh sage or 2 teaspoons dried sage
2 tablespoons finely chopped parsley
2 garlic cloves, minced (about 2 teaspoons)
1 teaspoon finely grated lemon zest

Preheat oven to 400°F.

Peel root vegetables and cut into 3-inch matchsticks,
between ½- and ¾-inch thick. Place in large bowl, add
olive oil, and toss until vegetables are evenly coated.
Season with salt and sage.

Transfer vegetables to large roasting pan where they can
fit without overlapping. Roast 20 minutes, mix well, and
continue roasting until crispy outside and tender inside,
about 40 minutes total. The harder root vegetables will
take longer to cook than the potatoes. Toss with parsley,
garlic, and lemon zest.

Chapter 14

THE PRACTICE OF FOOD

"Am I fat?"

I've never actually asked this question of another human being—until now.

I'm sitting in the office of Dr. Linda Bacon, a nutrition professor in the Biology Department at City College of San Francisco and author of *Health at Every Size.* I'm here because I embrace the message of her book: don't wait to live your life, the perfect one you imagine you'll live one day in your perfect body. Live it now.

"Yes."

I want to make sure I've heard correctly. "You just said I'm fat, right?"

She nods and says again, "Yes."

I'm silent. My hitherto unspoken weight hierarchy always began with thin, moved on to average, then on to chunky, then on to fat, and then finally obese. I have always put myself in the chunky category, or its kinder, gentler cousin—curvy. But never fat. Fat is another country, far away from where I live.

After a pause she asks, "What does that mean to you?"

"Well, what the fuck does that mean to you?" I counter.

She remains calm. "Fat, you know," and here she grabs her nonexistent belly fat. "Adipose tissue. Fat."

That's it? "All you mean by fat is 'adipose tissue'?"

"Yes," she says, "that's all I mean. But I know it's a loaded term," she adds.

You might say that.

Bacon tells me that even though she's using the word *fat* in the most clinical sense, the truth is, labels are always arbitrary. One person's average is another person's fat is another person's curvy. So don't get hung up on the labels.

"So tell me again what you mean by calling me fat?" I ask.

"What I'm saying is you have adipose tissue I might not see on a thinner person." She pauses and then adds, "And regardless of any of these labels, you radiate health and vibrancy. I think you're gorgeous," she concludes.

I have to hand it to her; in our culture, *fat* and *gorgeous* are seldom used together in the same sentence.

Maybe she's using the word *fat* clinically, but it still stings. What's more, she's right. And I know it.

Couldn't I just accept this? Be fat and be fine with it? It's not that I yearn to look like a model. I'm heading toward 50, and I've had two children. I just know that at this point, for me, being fat doesn't feel good. My fat shows up in lots of ways: when I walk up hills and have to take frequent rests, when I need to buy the next size pants because my current ones don't close.

If I'm going to change, I need to see clearly. Bacon's words may cut, but they're helping me do that.

• • •

It's one thing to understand something in my mind and another to understand it in my body. And the only way I've ever been able to move from my mind to my body is through attention and practice. I've been doing yoga for a long time and thought I knew this already.

I'm fat. My portions are out of balance. After all my explorations of different foods and my trips outward and inward, I still eat too much.

Everything I've wanted in life I've had to practice to achieve. Finding the right relationship with food is no different. I couldn't see that a year ago. Now it's in my face. And there's no room left for me to dodge it.

There's a practice for each of us. As a cook, I've always preferred tossing and improvising to carefully measuring out ingredients. As a person, I've always felt it was my right to eat as much as I want, whenever I want. Now, my practice will be measuring my food.

• • •

This is a portion?

I'm weighing out three ounces of salmon. It's about the size of my palm—excluding my fingers. I'm cooking dinner; and while Scott makes tortellini for the boys, I'm making baked salmon topped with lemon and dill for myself, along with brown rice and heaps of sautéed kale. I measure out a cup of rice, which, by the way, is about the size of my fist. The three ounces of salmon seems small compared to what I'm used to, but what I'm used to was too much.

As my family chows down on their tortellini (topped with excellent parmesan cheese from The Cheese Board), I eat my wild salmon. It's fresh, and the oily flesh is satisfying. I eat my cup of nutty brown rice along with my kale. When I'm done, I'm neither hungry nor full. I'm satisfied, and that is unfamiliar.

My routines are changing now. When I make a salad, I take five olives out of the jar, and I add olive oil by the teaspoon instead of pouring it on. I sauté greens and top them with four ounces of grilled chicken. I take one square of chocolate, not the entire bar. I treat myself to a small piece of Acme Bread baguette with an ounce of triple-cream Cambozola cheese, not the wedge. And I still eat the most delicious yogurt in the world, from Straus Creamery, but now I have half a cup, not a heaping bowl.

And I follow the advice of Linda Prout, a nutritionist based in Eugene, Oregon, whom I interviewed for a magazine piece many years ago. I add Celtic sea salt to my food, because it's full of minerals such as iron, magnesium, and potassium. I eat small, oily fish like sardines, herring, and anchovies, because of their high levels of omega-3 oils, and make sure to eat lots of cooked vegetables, especially leafy greens.

I not only measure my food, I also write down everything I eat. It is the only way I make sure that I don't trick myself and that I'm accountable. I've stopped fantasizing that I can find balance without paying close attention to quantity. Maybe one day I won't have to measure and record, because understanding what a reasonable portion is will be second nature. But not now and maybe not for a long time.

I pay attention to words, because words have power. I don't say I'm on a diet; rather, I think of measuring as a practice. Just like going to my yoga mat is practice. Practice is what you do every day to achieve what you desire. To write a book, you practice writing. You sit down each day, and you do the work.

It is no different with losing weight. One ounce of triple-cream Cambozola may be a small amount, but an ounce is an ounce. A cup of rice is a cup of rice. This is what the singer in my dream meant when she said, "The secret is there is no secret." A portion is a portion, and practice is practice. There are no shortcuts.

Measuring, by its nature, requires me to pay attention to every portion. Measuring forms a container for my longings and boundaries for my lust. Without boundaries, I cannot find balance. Without limits, I cannot hope to be free.

Weeks, then months pass. I lose weight—5 pounds, 10 pounds, then 20, then more. I start buying clothes one size smaller, then another size smaller.

Even at this stage of my journey, I can see that being in a lighter body is complicated. I weigh less, but I am still left with myself. Weight can obscure many things, including lust, sadness, loneliness, anxiety, and anger. As I lose weight and my buffer loosens, I am forced to grapple with these states more directly. I practice patience—it takes the body and the mind time to learn to move through the world in a different way.

I know that my practice of food measurement is hardly an uncommon approach. I compare notes with friends, and I visit some of the different groups that support people who are trying to eat more carefully. I go to a Weight Watchers meeting; and I hear a 300-pound woman start to cry, saying she can't bear to go to her high-school reunion because she's "larger than a whale." Then I sit in an Overeaters Anonymous meeting and hear a 120-pound woman cry about her imperfect body. She ate chocolate the other week and, that night, rammed her stomach into a banister to try to force the food up.

It is a revelation to me that a 120-pound person and a 300-pound person can be similarly sad about their bodies. The thinner person may look like her act is more together, but pain is pain. Regardless of the number on the scale, few of us are truly happy and at home in the skin we're in.

In our culture, the number on the scale enforces a cruel hierarchy. Weight separates the worthy from the unworthy. But the truth is, it's difficult to be in a body, period. Witnessing this in myself and in others, I've begun to see through the delusion so many of us share—that when we reach a particular weight, we will automatically be happy.

Now I have an answer to the question that yoga teacher Patricia Walden asked me a decade ago. "Why are you in this body? What does it have to teach you?"

I've learned that my mind and my body are equals, that they are completely entwined, and that each needs the other's intelligence and wisdom to be whole. And I've learned that consciousness may be the beginning of transformation, but consciousness in action continues it.

My friend Timothy told me that it's possible to achieve absolute transformation very slowly. I believe him.

So I'm taking the long view. I have no goal for my weight. I spent so many years out of balance that it's hubris to believe achieving a number will mean I've found it. I am curvy by design, and I praise that! I'm not trying to look like anyone else; I'm trying to become more myself.

I am in a bardo state, as Bo Forbes described. I'm in the process of letting go of old patterns, with new ones starting to emerge. I'm not sure where I'll land. But I keep measuring my food, and slowly, I'm waking up, meeting myself as I am, not who I wish I was.

I do my practice. I keep showing up.

• • •

Kale Chips

1 head kale, any kind you like
1½ tablespoons olive oil
2 teaspoons toasted sesame seeds
1 teaspoon Celtic sea salt

Preheat oven to 250°F.

Strip kale off stems and tear roughly into chip-size pieces. (You should have about 6 cups.) Rinse and spin dry. Lay kale out on paper towels, and pat completely dry.

Place kale in a bowl, and toss with olive oil. Lay out in one even layer on 2 baking sheets.

Bake 20–25 minutes or until crisp, stirring occasionally. Grind sesame seeds with salt in coffee grinder. Sprinkle over kale and serve.

Chapter 15

THE OFFERING OF FOOD

There's habitual hunger, where no matter how much you eat, you're still hungry for something more. Then there's actual hunger, where you don't have enough to eat and aren't sure where your next meal will come from.

For the last year, I've journeyed into my relationship with food in order to find balance. Through it all, I've had enough to eat. My struggle is one of abundance, not lack.

I'm standing in the kitchen of the Dorothy Day House in Berkeley, surrounded by the smell of cheap cooking oil and chlorine bleach. I'm here with other volunteers from a local synagogue to cook dinner for about 50 guests of the Berkeley Men's shelter. I'm here because I know that working with the real hunger of others has something to teach me.

We have two hours to prep before we serve dinner. When I'm told what the menu is, I feel like I've stepped into the pages of an old Betty Crocker cookbook: turkey meatloaf with barbeque sauce, string bean casserole with condensed mushroom soup and canned onion rings, instant mashed potatoes, and a salad with Thousand Island dressing.

The turkey meatloaf will take the longest, so that's where the volunteers begin. One chops several pounds of onions, then throws them on the grill with copious amounts of cooking oil from a large yellow plastic jug.

Two other volunteers, a mother and her ten-year-old son, begin opening packages of ground turkey meat, about 12 pounds in all. They dump the meat into a large metal bowl and start kneading it with their hands. I almost gag. I don't eat turkey, and seeing all that raw chopped meat turns my stomach. I watch as they add eggs, bread crumbs, and Worcestershire sauce and continue to knead. When the onions are done, they are added to the meat mixture.

Ronna Kabatznick, a congregation member, is in charge of the string bean casserole. It was Ronna, an assistant clinical professor at the Langley Porter Psychiatric Institute at the University of California–San Francisco and author of *The Zen of Eating,* who invited me to join this group of monthly volunteers. I start opening two six-pound cans of beans with a rusty can opener, the only one I can find. It's slow going. I'm not sure if this old can opener has the power to open these giant cans. Another volunteer finds an industrial-size can opener, saving my fingers and wrists.

After I drain the beans, Ronna throws them into a huge metal pan. She pours what looks like more than a gallon of gloppy cream-of-mushroom soup over them and mixes it all together with a large metal spoon.

"I'm glad you're here," she says to me as she tops the casserole with canned onion rings. "These people will eat what they get, appreciate it, and won't complain. There's a freedom in that. Service stuns people into realizing they have abundance."

She's right. Just a few days ago, I had lunch with a wealthy friend. We went out to a good restaurant; and when her starter came, focaccia with caramelized onion and goat cheese, she took one bite of it, then threw it down, saying, "It's soaked in oil," and shoved it aside.

I had no problem with her not liking it. But I did with her derisive attitude toward her food, and with wasting an entire plate of it because it wasn't exactly to her liking. It's one thing to have a choice, another to realize it, and still another to be grateful for it.

On the other side of the kitchen, I see the turkey meatloaf shaping up. The mother and son form the meat into 12 one-pound football-shaped loaves, pour barbeque sauce over the top of each, and pop the trays into the oven.

One volunteer opens some bags of premade salad into a big bowl, while two others cut baguettes down the middle and slather them with margarine and garlic powder for garlic bread. I begin the mashed potatoes.

I open the five-pound bag of instant potato flakes, then heat a vat of milk along with a big lump of margarine in a big pot on the stove. I have an atavistic fondness for instant mashed potatoes: when I was young, my mother used to mix them with a can of spinach and melted margarine. I thought they were delicious.

When the milk and margarine are warm, I pour the flakes in and watch as they disappear into the liquid. Within a few seconds, the potatoes are done. I cover the pot and turn off the flame.

Dinner begins in 15 minutes. I leave the kitchen and go into the large room where we will be serving. Everything seems to be the same dingy white color—the linoleum floor, the ceiling, the fluorescent lights, the Formica tables. Men are milling about, most of them middle-aged and African American. Some watch TV on the other side of the room, a few play cards, and some just sit.

I place red vinyl tablecloths over the two long serving tables. The synagogue brings them because they want the tables to look nice. Another volunteer brings out paper plates, napkins, plastic forks, spoons, and knives and sets them up at either end of each table, so the men can form two lines and be fed more quickly. They start to hover near the tables—their hunger is palpable.

I head back into the kitchen, where the turkey meatloaf has been taken out of the oven. Praise the transformative powers of cooking! The loaves are now nicely browned and look a lot better than they did an hour ago. I'm told to cut each loaf into ten slices, but I decide to cut only eight slices per loaf, so the men can have bigger pieces.

We bring out the trays of food, putting the turkey loaves at both ends of each table, along with the garlic bread. The salad bowl, green-bean casserole, and pot of mashed potatoes sit in the center.

The men form lines at the end. Some move briskly, others with dejected gaits and the hung heads of the longtime poor.

No one takes food here—all are served. At first I think this is to avoid hoarding. But then I'm told that Dorothy Day, the Catholic social activist for whom these centers across the country are named, believed that serving the poor is a kind of spiritual practice, conferring dignity and respect not only on the person being fed but also on the person doing the feeding.

Just as I'm about to serve my first piece of meatloaf, a young man, probably in his 20s, stands up and shouts out, "Wait a minute! We haven't said grace."

Most of the men in the room bow their heads, as do I along with the other volunteers. People begin to murmur the Lord's Prayer. These men have so little but are still grateful. I feel sad. Eating should be a basic human right, not an act of generosity.

As I put slices of meatloaf on their plates, they thank me, often with a smile. One man asks me for the burnt end of the meatloaf, and I laugh. "I like the burnt ends of things, too," I tell him. I begin to cut an end piece; and he says that he doesn't mean to be rude, but would I mind if he had the piece at the *other* end of the *other* loaf? "It's more burnt," he says. I'm glad to oblige.

"How you doing?" says a man to me as I'm about to serve him. Then, without waiting for an answer, he moves on.

As I'm about to serve the next man in line, he says, "No, thank you, I'm a vegetarian." The volunteers next to me give him an extra helping of mashed potatoes and two pieces of garlic bread.

The men sit down at the room's many round tables and eat. There is little talk but a lot of chewing. When the last man is served, we survey the serving trays for more food. There is enough to give people a second helping.

"There's more food here if anyone is still hungry," a volunteer calls out. Some men begin to line up again. I apologize to one man because I only have broken pieces of meatloaf to give him. "No need to apologize," he says. "I'm the father of six; I know what it's like to eat what's left over. This is good. I'm blessed."

As I serve him some broken pieces, I realize something: just as there is a crisis of hunger in the world, there is also a crisis of desire—where you're always hungry, whether it's for food, or things, or attention, or admiration. There's no end to wanting more—until you recognize the abundance you already have. My search for balance extends beyond food. It extends to all that I am attached to and all I consume. I have to say "no" to some things so I can say "yes" to others. Each decision to consume is a choice to spend my time, energy, and attention. Maybe one key to being happier is not having more, but needing less.

I hand the man his meatloaf. He thanks me, and I serve the next man in line.

String Bean Casserole

Serves 6

2 pounds washed green beans, ends trimmed, cut into thirds
2 tablespoons unsalted butter
1 onion, sliced thinly in rings (about 1 cup)
1 pound mushrooms, any kind you prefer, cleaned
    and sliced
1 cup cream
¾ cup chicken stock
1 tablespoon chopped fresh thyme or 1 teaspoon dried
    thyme
⅔ cup grated Parmesan cheese
½ teaspoon paprika
Salt and pepper to taste

Preheat oven to 350°F.

Blanch green beans in boiling water for 3–4 minutes,
removing them while they are still crisp. Drain, then
rinse under cold water.

Heat butter in large skillet over medium-high heat and
add onions. Cook 3–5 minutes, then add mushrooms.
Cook about 10 minutes or until both are soft. Add cream,
chicken stock, and thyme. Season to taste with salt and
pepper and cook on medium heat for about 10 minutes.
Add green beans and stir to coat.

Pour mixture into greased 13-by-9-inch baking dish.
Sprinkle first with Parmesan, then paprika on top. Bake
40 minutes until nicely browned on top.

Chapter 16

ORANGES

Oranges are among my favorite fruits. I love how the juice squirts out when you bite into a section and how they can be both sweet and sour and taste like the sun.

My family and I are driving north to Blue Heron Farm, an organic 20-acre farm in Rumsey, California, about 100 miles north of where we live. It is just two days before the winter solstice, and the sky is soft with light from the weak southerly sun.

As we head into the Sacramento Valley, we hit tule fog, the low-lying fog that can hover around these parts in the winter. We turn on the headlights and drive on.

Some places, like this orchard, call to me. At the end of my complicated journey, I'm drawn to a simple pleasure— eating a ripe orange right off a tree.

On Interstate 80, we're passed by a Harley-Davidson-riding Hell's Angel wearing a Santa Claus hat. The land is green from winter rain. Scott brings one of his great music mixes; and we listen to everything from Dion and the Belmonts to the Talking Heads, Dire Straits, and Creedence Clearwater Revival. We hit Interstate 505 and begin passing orchards filled with neatly laid rows of nut trees. After more than an hour, we enter the Capay Valley. Horses dot the landscape while hawks soar above. We pass Full Belly Farm, where the boys and I visited this past summer, its fields filled with giant purple cabbages. We drive a few miles farther, then turn down a rough, rocky road and into Blue Heron.

We pull up and park in front of a packing shed. John Ceteras, who owns Blue Heron along with his wife, Gretchen, comes out to greet us. He tells us he has just an hour. It's been a rough week. A cold front came through a few days ago and temperatures in the Capay Valley dropped as low as 18 degrees. With a round-the-clock effort, he and his farm crew managed to save the fruit. Even still, it's a small crop this year.

"We're praying for rain," he says. A lot of it he says, enough to "get the ground wet way down deep." The trees need that to produce a good crop.

In a good year, a tree can yield 200 to 300 pounds of fruit. "But look over there," John says, pointing toward his main navel orange orchard. "You should see a wall of oranges, but instead, it's spotty." He's right. Some trees are fuller than others, but I can see a lot of green. "We'll have 20 percent of our navel crop this year," he says grimly. Navel oranges are his most profitable fruit, selling for $2 a pound at farmers' markets.

As we head toward the orchards, John tells me he grows all kinds of citrus—limes, lemons, blood oranges, Rio Blanco and ruby red grapefruits, navel and Valencia oranges, and Mandarins—both Satsuma and Clementine. As we walk, we pass an old Eureka lemon bush. I hardly ever eat Eurekas anymore, since the smaller, sweeter Meyer lemon came into vogue. "May I?" I ask. John nods, and I twist one off its stem and place it in my pocket.

We reach the navel orange orchard, and I see that the edges of many of the leaves are brown. "Frost burn," John explains. We walk in and out of the rows, and I notice that some trees are full of oranges on one side but not the other. John shrugs. It's a mystery he can't fully explain.

Most of the oranges grow in clusters, some with up to a dozen fruits. Even on just one tree, there is great difference among the fruits. Some of the oranges have smooth skin, some wrinkly. Some are small, others enormous.

Matthew reaches his hand into one particularly prolific tree and looks at John. I know what he wants—to grab one of those oranges and twist it off. And, since he's a boy, not just to grab it but to vanquish it. I understand—the oranges are alluring, like edible Christmas ornaments. I share his fruit lust but am trying to keep mine in check.

John nods and Matthew twists—and twists and twists. "Maybe it doesn't want to come off?" I venture.

"Here," John says, "try this one." Matthew reaches to another branch, grabs a wrinkly orange, and twists. It falls into his hand.

John takes out a well-used pocketknife; and as he cuts through the skin to the fruit, the sweet aroma of orange fills the air. Such a happy smell! He hands each of us a segment and we taste. It's sweet, and a hint of tang hits the sides of my mouth and the back of my tongue. It is full of life and utterly delicious. As I take a bite, I remember what Eric, the Zen chef, said when I started this journey: that when you eat an orange, "which is sweet and tastes like sunshine . . . don't only let your mouth respond. Let your heart respond." Mine does. I feel so happy eating this orange, I can't help believing that the earth must have known that in winter we might need cheering up, and given us these sweet orbs as a gift.

We wend our way through more of the orchard, past a 100-year-old fuyu persimmon tree and toward the packing shed. As we walk, I see a pallet of gigantic gourds. "Gretchen is a gourd artist," John says. "She lusts for gourds, so I grow them for her. It's my gift to her." I think, but don't say out loud, that this is one of the most romantic things I've ever heard.

I ask if I can see some of her work; and all of us, along with Sienna, the farm's exuberant pit-bull mix, head toward the house.

I feel like I've stepped into Santa's workshop. The piney scent of a Christmas tree greets us upon entry. Gretchen's studio is off to the right, and she sits at a wooden workbench brushing iridescent paint onto small gourds, which will soon become Christmas ornaments.

Gretchen takes us through a set of glass doors into the dining room that also serves as a showroom. The table and shelves are filled with the deep amber glow of gourds in all shapes and sizes. Some are plain, while others are etched with black wood-burned designs. Some are musical instruments and others are all manner of vases and pots. I like the fact that they are not only beautiful —they are also useful. Jack picks one gourd up, starts to shake it like a maraca, and breaks into a big smile.

Gretchen tells us that every gourd has a story. "I look at its shape and utility. After I clean off the skin, I can see the patterns. Sometimes I'll spend days just looking at them. Sometimes I work out designs with a pencil and it just doesn't work. It doesn't feel right. So I do it again.

"It's my job to see the story in each gourd," she adds. "I just bring out what's already there."

We buy some gourds to take home, thank Gretchen for her time, and start back to our car. Along the way we pass an old grapefruit tree. "It's over 100 years old," John says. He pulls off a fruit and hands it to me.

As we say good-bye, he suggests we drive a dozen miles up the road into the canyon. "There've been a few bald eagle sightings," he says. I doubt it. Bald eagles are usually found farther north, in Washington State and Alaska, and farther east, in the Rocky Mountains. But we're game.

We drive west along Highway 16. It's beautiful. The winter sun is just starting to emerge from the clouds. As we drive, I think about Gretchen's gourds and how she looks for the truth in every gourd's form. This, in essence, is what this past year's journey has been—to learn what my form has to teach me and to find what is true within me.

I see that my body, with its generous curves and flesh, is not perfect. But it is still beautiful, and I am grateful to it. With it, I gave birth to our children and hold my husband in my arms. With it, I cook the food that nourishes us, do yoga, sing, and write these words.

Weight can be gained or lost. Our judgments about our bodies are much harder to lose. I see that my body is strong. It lets me do things both beautiful and practical. I am grateful to have found a practice that is helping me find balance and lose weight. But the scale is a witness to my journey, not the measure of my worth. It is with gratitude and humility that I am learning to take care of my body, because it is the embodiment of my spirit and the vehicle with which I make my way through this complicated, magnificent world.

"A great horned owl!" Matthew says, interrupting my reverie. I look, and just ahead, sitting by the side of the road, is a handsome owl with brown feathers, tufted ears, yellow eyes, and a swiveling head. As our car approaches, the owl takes flight into the trees.

I love owls. They are such strange, beautiful birds of prey. Even if we don't see an eagle, seeing this owl is more than enough.

We drive on into Cache Creek Regional Park, down the loopy, windy road. During this year, excavating my eating history has given me compassion for the girl I was. Working with food artisans has given me respect for the talent it takes to create beautiful food. Visiting farms and orchards has shown me the immense hard work that goes into growing food and given me a deeper appreciation for what I eat. Watching steer get slaughtered has made me realize that eating meat is a grave choice, one never to be made lightly. Going back to the place I was born has laid old ghosts to rest. Going without food has taught me that cravings pass. Doing my yoga practice teaches me that my mind and body are intimately integrated. Measuring my food helps me find balance. Feeding hungry people shows me how abundant my life is. Maybe I've become less romantic about food, but I've also become more grateful for it.

I did all this to free myself, to wake up, because the world needs whatever I can give back to it. Because this is not a dress rehearsal and there is no time to waste. And if I still need to be reminded of some of these things, if I'm still a work in progress, it's because I'm a life in progress.

We drive on; and after a few more minutes, I tell Scott to turn the car around. I ate an orange off a tree; we saw an owl. I'm happy. It's enough.

We're pulling off the road to turn around when suddenly Matthew cries out, "A bald eagle! Over there!" Scott parks, and we get out of the car. I follow Matthew's pointing arm but don't see anything.

"Where is it?" I ask. "I can't see it."

"There, by the creek, on top of that tree," he says.

And sure enough, sitting on a branch about 20 yards away is an American bald eagle. It sits in profile, looking just as strong and free as it does on the back of a $1 bill.

The bird swivels its head toward us. He's as fierce a predator as I've ever seen, and that includes the mountain lion I saw near Yosemite National Park. He regards us as we regard him. After a few moments, he unfurls his wings into a giant six-foot span and, with one powerful flap, takes off down the creek bed.

"Would you look at that," I say. We are all quiet as we watch the eagle disappear into the canyon. That this bird is here at all, and no longer on the endangered-species list, fills me with hope for our future. We get back into the car and head for home.

Winter is almost upon us; but after that, the days will get longer again, and the sky will be more light than dark. The weather will get warmer, and life will bloom.

Maybe I'll plant some carrots and greens in our backyard. The boys can help me. The sun will shine, the plants will grow, and spring will come.

• • •

Orange

One lovely orange that calls your name

Cut orange lengthwise into six segments. Breathe in the aroma that's released. Eat each segment slowly, savoring the orange's flavor, taste, and texture.

Let it fill your mouth, and your heart, with joy.

Notes

Notes

Notes

Notes

Notes

Notes

Acknowledgments

Many people, in many ways, have supported me in my life and in this project. I'd like to thank:

John Abbott, Tina Barbaria, Davina Baum, Margo Bistis, Celine Bleu, Alice Bokankowitz, Lisa Buchberg, Kim Chernin, Deborah Cohan, Max Cowan, Charity Ferreira, Andrea Ferretti, Patricia Fox, Margit Frendberg, Robin Gianattasio-Malle, Sharon Goldfarb, Noreen Buyers Greenblatt, Sue Halpern, Vivian Ho, Richard Kahn, Rebecca Kaminsky, Mollie Katzen, Mignon Khargie, Rachel Klayman, Sarah Kleinman, Khatuna Kobiashvili, Jaime Kyle, Renee LaRose, John Leonardi, Bobbie Lewis, Lisa Litman, Marta Lostaunau, Elana Maggal, Karen Mates, Timothy McCall, Amy Moon, Ginny Morgan, Bill Morris, Kate Moses, Holly Pope, Audrey Pratt, Linda Prout, Yvonne Rand, Amy Rappaport, Beth Rashbaum, Tracy Ross, Melissa Ong Ryan, Michael Salveson, Rachel Sarah, Hale Sofia Schatz, Robyn Scheer, Denise Shapiro, Stephanie Snyder, Kim Capelouto Sorrell, Naomi Starkman, Charlene Stern, Michael Tompkins, Laurie Marks Wagner, Jennifer Ward, Jake Warner, Phil Wood, and Alexandra Zeigler. Also the following organizations: Congregation Netivot Shalom, Dorothy Day House of

Berkeley, the Hoffman Institute, Overeaters Anonymous, Weight Watchers, Tehiyah Day School, and *Yoga Journal* magazine.

My yoga teachers, past and present—I am grateful for your knowledge and wisdom: Karl Erb, Bo Forbes, Ana Forrest, Evlaleah Howard, Sri B. K. S. Iyengar, Judith Hanson Lasater, Tias Little, Saranna Miller, Aadil Palkhivala, Richard Rosen, and Patricia Walden. I am especially grateful to Scott Blossom for his tenacity, kindness, and skill.

All those who opened up their farms, gardens, ranches, hearts, and minds and made this book possible: Linda Bacon, Bill Briscoe, Scott Brennan, Clive Brown and Malena Lopez-Maggi, Edward Espe Brown, Carolla Dost, Chandra Easton, Eric Green, Joan Gussow, Ronna Kabatznick, Craig Long, Joanna Macy, Iso Rabins, Abbie Scianamblo, and Mike "Bone Daddy" Thomas. Also John Ceteras and Gretchen Ceteras of Blue Heron Farm; John McDowell and Alexandra Spadea of Camp Hill Farm and the Rockland Farm Alliance; Linda Concklin of the Orchards of Concklin; Andrew Brait, Paul Muller, Judith Redmond, and Dru Rivers of Full Belly Farm; McEvoy Ranch; Mary Rickert, Jim Rickert, James Rickert, Mark Estes, Scott Towne, and the crew at Prather Ranch; David Bice, Jennifer Bice, Erika Scharfen, and Trinity Smith of Redwood Hill Farm; Mac Mead, Lory Widmer, and the staff of the Threefold community.

The artists who have moved and inspired me: Joni Mitchell, Neil Young, Richard Thompson, Van Morrison, Roger McGuinn, John Lennon, Joan Baez, Bob Dylan, the New Pornographers, Stevie Wonder, Philip Pullman, Lucille Ball, Matt Groening, Hal Ashby and Cat Stevens for *Harold and Maude,* and Hayao Miyazaki for all his films, but especially for *Spirited Away.*

Patty Gift, my editor at Hay House, for her faith, and for giving me the freedom to let this book become what it wanted.

My agent, Stephanie Tade, who supported me when *Ravenous* was just an idea, and who told me, "The best books are the most brave."

Louise Hay, founder of Hay House; Reid Tracy, president and CEO of Hay House, who said "yes"; Sally Mason, Laura Koch, Anne Barthel, Jacqui Clark, Lindsay McGinty, and the rest of the Hay House team.

Kathryn Arnold, for her early encouragement.

Kelle Walsh, for her early edits that helped hone my words.

Fiona Kennedy, recipe tester par excellence.

Pearl Mayer, my sixth grade teacher who inspired me to live big.

Pamela Brown Shore, for her generous heart and long friendship.

Kaitlin Quistgaard, for reminding me what's important.

Robyn Macy, my sister and best friend, who has my back and makes me laugh.

My family: David Macy, Todd Macy, Jean and Coleman Rosenberg, Kyra Macy Kaufman, Lindsey Kaufman Robertson, Doug Robertson, Paul Rowe, Zarin Arab, and Harris Jacobs.

Bruno Wassertheil, with gratitude for giving my mother the happiest years of her life.

My grandparents, Jacob and Celia Bogoff and Joseph and Ellen Macy, my aunts, Loretta Bogoff Friedman and Betty Bogoff Fishbein, and my uncle, Phillip Fishbein.

My father, Gilbert Macy—I miss your luminous and brave spirit.

My mother, Estelle Bogoff Macy, for her strength and love, and for teaching me that worrying in advance occasionally has merit.

My sons, Matthew and Jack, whom I love more than I can express in words—I am so proud to be your mother.

And finally, Scott, always my first reader, whose brilliant edits made this a better book, and in whose fierce mind and generous soul I've made my home.

About the Author

Dayna Macy's essays have appeared in *Self, Salon .com, Yoga Journal,* and other publications, as well as several anthologies. For the last decade she has worked at *Yoga Journal* as communications director, and she is now also the managing editor for international editions. She lives in Berkeley, California, with her husband, the writer Scott Rosenberg, and their two sons.

Website: **www.daynamacy.com**

Hay House Titles of Related Interest

YOU CAN HEAL YOUR LIFE, the movie,
starring Louise L. Hay & Friends
(available as a 1-DVD program
and an expanded 2-DVD set)
Watch the trailer at: **www.LouiseHayMovie.com**

THE SHIFT, the movie,
starring Dr. Wayne W. Dyer
(available as a 1-DVD program
and an expanded 2-DVD set)
Watch the trailer at: **www.DyerMovie.com**

• • •

*THE SPARK: The 28-Day Breakthrough Plan
for Losing Weight, Getting Fit, and
Transforming Your Life,* by Chris Downie

*THE CORE BALANCE DIET:
4 Weeks to Boost Your Metabolism and
Lose Weight for Good,* by Marcelle Pick

*EXCUSES BEGONE!: How to Change Lifelong,
Self-Defeating Thinking Habits,* by Dr. Wayne W. Dyer

*LIGHTEN UP!: The Authentic and Fun Way to Lose
Your Weight and Your Worries,* by Loretta LaRoche

• • •

All of the above are available at your local bookstore,
or may be ordered by contacting Hay House (see next page).

We hope you enjoyed this Hay House book. If you'd like
to receive our online catalog featuring additional information
on Hay House books and products, or if you'd like to find
out more about the Hay Foundation, please contact:

Hay House, Inc., P.O. Box 5100, Carlsbad, CA 92018-5100
(760) 431-7695 or (800) 654-5126
(760) 431-6948 (fax) or (800) 650-5115 (fax)
www.hayhouse.com® • **www.hayfoundation.org**

• • •

Published and distributed in Australia by: Hay House Australia Pty.
Ltd., 18/36 Ralph St., Alexandria NSW 2015 • *Phone:* 612-9669-4299
Fax: 612-9669-4144 • www.hayhouse.com.au

Published and distributed in the United Kingdom by:
Hay House UK, Ltd., 292B Kensal Rd., London W10 5BE • *Phone:*
44-20-8962-1230 • *Fax:* 44-20-8962-1239 • www.hayhouse.co.uk

Published and distributed in the Republic of South Africa by:
Hay House SA (Pty), Ltd., P.O. Box 990, Witkoppen 2068 • *Phone/Fax:*
27-11-467-8904 • info@hayhouse.co.za • www.hayhouse.co.za

Published in India by: Hay House Publishers India, Muskaan
Complex, Plot No. 3, B-2, Vasant Kunj, New Delhi 110 070 • *Phone:*
91-11-4176-1620 • *Fax:* 91-11-4176-1630 • www.hayhouse.co.in

Distributed in Canada by: Raincoast, 9050 Shaughnessy St.,
Vancouver, B.C. V6P 6E5 • *Phone:* (604) 323-7100
Fax: (604) 323-2600 • www.raincoast.com

• • •

<u>Take Your Soul on a Vacation</u>

Visit **www.HealYourLife.com®** to regroup, recharge,
and reconnect with your own magnificence.
Featuring blogs, mind-body-spirit news, and life-changing
wisdom from Louise Hay and friends.

Visit **www.HealYourLife.com** today!